STAGE II RELATIONSHIPS

STAGE II RELATIONSHIPS

Love Beyond Addiction

Earnie Larsen

HarperOne
An Imprint of HarperCollinsPublishers

HarperOne

HarperCollins books may be purchased for educational, business, or sales promotional use. For information, please e-mail the Special Markets Department at SPsales@harpercollins.com.

HarperCollins Web site: http://www.harpercollins.com

HarperCollins®, 📖®, and HarperOne™ are trademarks of HarperCollins Publishers.

Library of Congress Cataloging-in-Publication Data

Larsen, Earnest.
  Stage II relationships.

  Includes index.
  1. Alcoholics—Family relationships. 2. Alcoholics—Psychology. I. Title. II. Title: Stage 2 Relationships.
III. Title: Stage two relationships.
HV5132.L37   1987
362.2'92   86-45815
ISBN: 978–0–06–254808–5

HB 12.04.2017

To Dewey and Peg,
Stage II people enjoying a Stage II relationship

And to three special women:
Sabrina, of the house of nails;
Kate, of Edina; and
Denise, who keeps the sky from falling in

CONTENTS

INTRODUCTION

Shortly after the publication of *Stage II Recovery: Life Beyond Addiction*, I became convinced of the need for a sequel on Stage II relationships. One of the messages of my previous book was that intimacy and relationships are the core of the whole recovery process. That book ended with a chapter on relationships, but I knew the subject deserved extended treatment.

If ever I had any doubts about the importance of intimacy, letters like this one convinced me of the need for this new book:

Dear Earnie:

I feel like I want and need to take some time and give you feedback on my personal journey of recovery. So much has been happening and I have made a commitment to keep in touch with the people who have been part of my journey.

After seven years of sobriety and God knows how many meetings, therapy sessions, and programs, I have come to the astounding conclusion that mostly I am lonely. All of my life there's been a glass wall between me and just about everyone I have ever had a relationship with. In a way, I have lots of friends—but they only go so far. The bottom line is, I end up alone, feeling alone, and thinking I deserve to be alone.

In a word, my relational skills have been zilch, whether the relationship is with God (who I know is unhappy with me), with men (who I know will leave me once they find out the truth), with my kids (who play my sense of guilt like a guitar), with my coworkers (who always take advantage of me), or just with life in general (it is never fair). More troublesome than any of these, of course, is my relationship with myself. I just never liked me very well and therefore never figured I deserved the really good things in life.

Treatment taught me how not to drink. It did not teach me how to live. And you know what? In the past seven years, I became a double winner and started going to Al-Anon; and then a triple winner by taking in quite a few Adult Children of Alcoholics meetings. I found that we may come from slightly different places, *but we are all the same.* The same living issues—exactly the same issues—keep surfacing in all these different kinds of meetings. We are all lonely. We are all stopped by the glass wall. We are all deficient in the skills we need to have healthy relationships.

So now my effort and energy in recovery are much more focused on getting rid of the glass wall. Slowly, because it is *so* scary, I am learning what I need to do to connect with others. Mostly it has to do with changing my own attitudes and perceptions. But I am learning, and my life is so much "warmer," so to speak, because I am getting closer to people.

Thanks for all your help. Your Stage II concepts are right on. At least they are for me where I am at. Thanks. If I ever meet you, I am counting on the glass wall not being there.

Jenny A.

What Is Recovery?

Stage II Recovery proposed that if we are ever to experience the fullness of our recovery potential, we need first to define what recovery means to us. Each individual's definition of recovery sets him or her on a clearly defined path. Although recovery is certainly a process or journey, rather than a destination, it is vitally important that we map out the direction our recovery will take.

I've asked thousands of recovering people what recovery means to them. Strangely enough, few people have a clear idea. Overwhelmingly, their definitions include vague and general terms such as "feeling better," "getting control of my life," and even "never allowing anyone ever to hurt me again." Sometimes they give me an utterly mystified look, as though any idiot knew the answer: "Recovery means being sober. What else could it mean?"

Stage I and Stage II

In dealing with recovery, I have found it important to distinguish clearly between Stage I recovery (breaking the primary addiction) and Stage II recovery (rebuilding the life that was saved in Stage I). They are sequential. One follows the other; or, in other words, one is necessary before the other. It is not that one is "good" and the other "better." The fact is that many people reach a dead end or plateau in their personal recovery; and if they do not understand what is occurring, they frequently feel they're "losing" their recovery. Everything that used to be so meaningful no longer is, and their new-found excitement and health no longer feel terrific. Not knowing how to handle this experience, they tend to get angry or depressed, or they slide into some form of switched addiction to compensate for their feelings of loss.

I've concluded that what may actually be happening is that they have simply reached the end of Stage I recovery. They have broken the power of the main addiction. Although they *could* slip back (we all can), for now they've quieted the old demons, dealt with the old issues fairly well, and achieved freedom from addiction.

I have often seen recovering people "stall" somewhere between the second and the sixth year of their program, and the effect can be devastating. They think, "I always believed that once I climbed this mountain, I'd be home free. How come I don't feel free?" The question I am asking is, "How *could* they feel free?" They have defined recovery as breaking the primary addiction; but once they do that, freedom still eludes them.

What they don't understand is that they are now facing the real mountain—the basic, fundamental issues that have been there all along, that were there before the addiction, that grew stronger as the addiction took control, and that still remain once Stage I freedom has been achieved.

Dealing with the mountain of living is what Stage II recovery is all about. It is about getting on with life by facing those patterns, habits, and attitudes that control your life and which, for perhaps the first time, you are clearheaded, sober, or emotionally sound enough to face. Stage I recovery is what makes it possible for a pilgrim to undertake the journey of Stage II recovery.

Defining Stage II

Because recovery needs to be specifically defined in order to be effective, and because Stage I recovery is defined as breaking the primary addiction, I have further defined Stage II recovery as "learning to love." That definition may appear to be simplistic, but it should not be taken lightly. What's more, it is important to understand that Stage II recovery is not an issue *only* for addicted persons. If Stage II means learning to love, we are all on that journey, and we all need to face the same issues of personal and spiritual growth.

All of us were made for love, and every movement of our hearts is an attempt to meet and fill that need in some way. Research has proven many times that we need intimacy in order to lead successful and happy lives. Babies who are denied physical contact with other people will die, even if their basic needs are met. Babies who sleep in hospital nurseries where the constant steady sound of a heartbeat is played over the intercom are far more calm and relaxed than babies in ordinary nurseries. At the other end of the life cycle, senility is not necessarily inevitable: It is often the result of a loss of meaning and purpose in life, a feeling that no one cares about us or considers us important. At all ages we need intimacy and love. Thus, a journey towards learning to love is important to everyone, not just those who have traveled through Stage I.

If the first principle of Stage II recovery is learning to love, then the second is that love exists only in relationships. No one simply *has* love. Martin Buber has written that "love exists between two poles creating at both ends"—that is, in relationships; to achieve a satisfying degree of intimacy in those relationships, each individual must possess adequate skills. Many people love, but they are still not capable of making their relationships work.

At seminars I often ask, "Do you think a nonrecovering alcoholic can love?" After some hesitation and mumbling, someone generally says, "Yeah, I guess so." But those who are recovering alcoholics are never slow to answer. They always boom out, "Of course," and go on to explain that they stayed drunk most of the time because when they were sober they had to feel the pain of hurting those they loved so much.

Then I ask another question. "Maybe they can love, but what can't they do?" The answer, of course, is that they can't make relationships work; and because they can't, they stay locked forever behind the glass wall that Jenny A. wrote about, wondering why they are so lonely.

But the nonrecovering alcoholic (sober or not) is not the only one who lacks the skills necessary to function in a healthy relationship. It is also the nonrecovering *anyone* who has not learned the skills necessary. Lacking these skills does not make us evil or bad; it simply prevents us from reaping the same benefits from our relationships that skilled people can.

The Core of Recovery

If Stage II recovery is learning to love, and if love exists only in relationships, then at the core of recovery is *becoming a person increasingly capable of functioning in a healthy relationship.* As you read this book, you will discover that you need to begin to understand and be willing to deal with yourself, not the other person. You'll discover that "who I am" has everything to do with the kind of relationship you enter into. "Who I am" affects what happens in your relationships and ultimately how you repeat the same pattern of your relationships throughout your life, unless *you* change something. No one has power or responsibility to change anyone else. The only person you can change is yourself.

Codependency Redefined

The term "codependency" gets bandied about a lot these days. Let the battle continue to rage over whether or not the term should apply only to those who have alcoholism in their background. For our purposes, let's just say that *codependency is caused by those self-defeating, learned behaviors that diminish our capacity to initiate or participate in loving relationships*. A satisfying relationship requires that each party comes to it with adequate self-esteem, sensitivity, and the ability to make a commitment. Each person must have a solid sense of his or her self apart from the other, so that each can lean without becoming dependent and have differences of opinion that don't lead to win-lose situations. For reasons that we will look into in more detail later, codependents have difficulty participating in loving, healthy relationships because they lack precisely the traits needed.

Wherever you have picked up the habits, perceptions, and attitudes that have hindered intimacy in your life, you need to deal with them. You must recover from them if you are ever going to be able to gain the skills necessary for healthy relationships. The living patterns that hinder us are present in everyone, whether we spend our time in A.A., Al-Anon, ACOA, or any of the other Twelve-Step groups around, or whether we're in a group at all. You don't have to come from a chemically dependent family or have a neurotic background to be in need of recovery. The important thing is what you learned when you were growing up, and all of us have learned some patterns that block our ability to share in the fullest intimacy possible.

The level of our capacity to share in loving relationships and to enjoy intimacy to the fullest is a good indicator of the success of our lives. Stage II recovery, upon which the success of our relationships depends, is therefore a matter of being willing and knowing how to deal with our particular type of codependency. Our codependency is our own personal, unique set of patterns and habits that continue to hinder our attempts at intimacy with others throughout our life.

This book will lay out some rules and principles and provide some charts and exercises designed to help you make relationships work. At the heart of this program, however, is the simple fact of human kindness. All these rules boil down to the need to extend ourselves to our partners in ways that make them feel special.

Many people enjoy happy, successful relationships but don't care about and could not enunciate a single principle this book is built upon. They don't have to. They are living the essential element— their partners know they care. They do the little things that count (and it's often the little things that are most important). Without any sort of training, they had the sensitivity to know what makes the difference, and they cared enough to do what was necessary.

On the other hand, countless others know just about everything there is to know about relationships—except how to enjoy them in their own lives. They're blocked. Somehow, somewhere, between the dream and the reality, as T. S. Eliot once wrote, falls the shadow. The shadow's name is codependency.

If all relationships were healthy and happy, this book would not be necessary; perhaps a book of love poetry would be more in order. But not all relationships are successful. Codependency, in fact, runs rampant in our society. Millions of people are miserable in their relationships and they don't know why, even though they've been acting out the same patterns all their lives.

That is why some rules and principles are necessary. They become still points—stakes that, once driven into the ground, offer marks against which we can measure ourselves, others, and the quality of our relationships. Human relationships are not built on objective rules, of course; they are about the subjective experience of loving. But the objective data is important, especially if we don't know why the same things keep happening to us over and over again.

That's the rationale of this book. It speaks to the need in each of us to love and be loved in the fullest, healthiest, most complete way. I invite you to join me in the "how" of Stage II relationships: a journey of exploring ourselves, understanding others, and learning to love.

Chapter 1

THERE ARE REASONS WHY

Because human beings are made to live in community, we are concerned with our relationships. The quality of our lives is determined by the quality of our relationships, whether with lovers, parents, friends, or coworkers. The same is true of our relationship with God (as we understand God to be), a relationship called faith.

But maintaining healthy, nurturing relationships is no small task. Often the problem is not only that a relationship causes us pain, but that *it keeps happening*. Either an ongoing relationship continually circles around to the same painful spot, or each new relationship ends up looking like the old ones. The frustrating part is that the same old things keep happening and we don't know why. So we feel helpless and hopeless about our ability ever to change.

Problems with relationships are especially common for people who grew up in dysfunctional homes—running the gamut from alcoholic to religiously neurotic environments. In homes like these, we learned profound messages: "What will the neighbors say?" "You made your bed, now lie in it." "Why can't you be a good little girl?" "Get tough, be a man, stop crying." "Work before you play." Long-forgotten lessons, but still profoundly active. We were bombarded with similar lessons about the importance of getting male approval, what we should do with our feelings, the priority of work, how to deal with anger, and what nurturing meant. We saw modeled for us how men and women were supposed to act, how adults dealt with conflict, and how people who cared about each other displayed their affection.

We learned, then we practiced, then we became what we practiced. As we grew older, we brought to *our* relationships exactly the perceptions and habits we saw practiced all our lives.

Reasons exist for whatever is going on in our relationships. The reasons are so plain and powerful that once we see them we have to admit that "there is no way it could be any different." Only when we understand those reasons can we make any decisions about them, and only on the heels of those decisions and the behavior that follows can we genuinely change. Things do not have to be as they always were.

A rather jolting (and sometimes revolting) rule of thumb is that *we become one parent and marry the other.* Here's a good way to test this principle in your own life: Write a brief sketch of the qualities of your parents' relationship (or the primary relationship you grew up with). Which parent got his or her own way? Who made the decisions? Who had the power? How was the power used? How were feelings treated? Jot down the phrases that your parents constantly used—the sayings you swore you would never say to *your* children.

Then, outline a similar sketch of your own primary relationship. In your relationship, who usually gets his or her way? Do you recognize any familiar patterns of manipulation? Are feelings handled in different ways than you saw modeled? And do you find yourself telling your children the same things your parents told you—and in the same tone of voice?

This mirroring of the past, this becoming one parent and marrying the other, does not necessarily follow gender lines. For any number of reasons, a woman may take on the primary qualities of her father. Maybe he was the quiet, passive one, and she was "daddy's little girl." Almost by osmosis, she became emotionally and spiritually like him. And perhaps the mother was the dominant, "bossy" one in the family. She always got her way, and the father submitted. If the daughter "becomes" her father, the odds are high that she will marry her "mother," a man who's dominant and bossy himself. She will hook up with someone who needs and demands that things be done his way (because it's the right way, of course).

This sort of emotional cloning can be played out many ways. Sons become fathers, daughters become mothers, or vice versa. And once we model ourselves on one person, we're propelled to find someone who fits our bill. There are always reasons.

To take the cycle one step further, do this: If you have children, write a similar sketch of each child's personality. Chances are, if you have more than one child, you'll discover that one tends to be a "me-first," "my-way-counts," "if-I-don't-get-my-way-I'll-pout-and-punish" sort of person. The other will tend to say "It's okay," "I don't want to get them mad," "What can I do to please them," "I don't understand what I'm supposed to do."

Your children will grow up mirroring what was modeled for them, and then they will pair off with other growing young people who fit their gaps. The cycle continues.

Of course, this process of mirroring and modeling is relative. Not everyone grew up in a dysfunctional family, and not all dysfunctional families are equally dysfunctional. The variety is infinite, so our own family histories and the quality of our current relationships will vary widely. You may find yourself in any one of the following situations:

- You are in a satisfying relationship. You want to improve what is already wonderful.
- You are not happy in your relationship. You want to know if a bad relationship can be saved. If it can, you want to know how to do it. What does it take?
- You are in a failed relationship. Your relationship is over, and you know it. You want to know how to end things, how to get closure. How do you end a relationship with no one getting hurt?

- You are single and have been for a long time. You may have been badly hurt in the past, and you want to know if you can ever trust again. How do you know when it's smart or safe?
- You are single but in a primary relationship. You like it but are scared to death, so your questions are about certitude. How can you tell if it's safe to go further? How do you ever know what's going on in another's head?

Obviously, no book can cover all of these topics. What we can do is present simple, honest, essential principles about relationships. And then, with the help of the exercises and charts that follow, you can apply the principles to your own life and learn more about the patterns and rules at work in your own relationship. These insights will give you the option to make effective decisions about how to change.

Driving Stakes

Let's begin by driving stakes that mark four basic principles about relationships:

1. Healthy people make healthy relationships.
2. Who you are in a relationship with says as much about you as it does about the other person.
3. Wherever you go, there you are.
4. If nothing changes, nothing changes.

Healthy People Make Healthy Relationships

No one, of course, is perfect, so no relationship is perfect. This first principle indicates that no relationship can be healthier than the people involved in it. As we shall see later, it is for this reason that the first commitment you make to a relationship should *not* be to the relationship itself but to your own personal growth. This is the starting point that can make toxic relationships safe and healthy relationships better.

Nancy's story perfectly illustrates this point:

Nancy is a thirty-seven-year-old mother of three. She is also an adult child of an alcoholic family. As she grew up, she learned that the only way for her to win the acceptance and approval she desperately wanted was to apologize. If she was sorry for how she behaved, she was a "good little girl," which is what she always wanted to be, since only good little girls were loved. She became an expert at feeling sorry and then expressing how sorry she was—for just about anything.

It was to her alcoholic father, however, that she most had to apologize, even if he wasn't present when she misbehaved or offended someone. She had learned that men counted more than women did, so apologies had to be made to males. It never dawned on Nancy that a man should ever apologize to her. Since her rights were not as important as a man's, he would never need to; he could never do anything bad enough to warrant an apology. Even though her father was abusive and punished her and others indiscriminately, Nancy soon got the picture that if she wanted him to hold her, she had to apologize to him whenever he was angry.

On some level, Nancy knew that she was blameless for her father's rages, but she continued to take the blame and say she was sorry. A volcano of anger built up in the young woman, but its explosive force was trapped under a rock mantle of passivity. It continually erupted, but no one knew because the tears were silent.

Mirroring her own parental pattern, Nancy then "became" her mother and married a man much like her father. Her husband was in the military and lived by the book of military discipline. He was a nice enough person, Nancy now says, but he always had to be right, and he was incapable of sharing his feelings or giving her the kind of nurturing love she needed. If her husband didn't get what he needed or wanted, he simply withdrew by ignoring her. True to her childhood pattern, Nancy would then admit that she was wrong, apologize, and be forgiven.

After ten years of marriage to this man, Nancy eventually began a recovery program. By now, her bottled-up rage was causing her physical and emotional problems, and the spillover was affecting her husband. The quality of their life together went from bad to worse.

But through the program Nancy discovered and began to understand some of the patterns that governed her life. She came to understand that she could not continue the dysfunctional patterns of her youth. She also learned to recognize that her husband's habits were just as long-lived and long-practiced as hers were, not mandates from on high. She came to understand that she was very much part of the problem, that the more she babied her husband and tolerated his intolerable behavior, the more permission she gave him to continue. As she realized the shape of the pattern of her marriage, she resented her part in perpetuating it.

As Nancy continued her recovery, she learned to first take care of herself. She stopped apologizing when it was not appropriate; she grew less and less dependent on getting approval from others; and she became more rooted in her own self-approval and self-esteem. Slowly, as a result of her Stage II recovery, she was able to share in and enjoy a Stage II relationship based on honesty, respect, and responsibility for her own growth.

It should be no surprise that Nancy's recovery at first greatly threatened her husband. As Nancy became more honest with him, he feared that she would find another man, believing that the reason she was unhappy with him was that he was inadequate and incapable of meeting her needs. This fear prompted extreme mood swings, temper tantrums, and frequent criticism of Nancy's efforts to change.

To the credit of each of them, however, they stayed toe-to-toe and eyeball-to-eyeball. They kept talking, and gradually their words began to make sense to each other. Nancy was able to affirm that she indeed loved her husband and that the last thing she wanted was for their marriage to fall apart. She was not in the market for another man.

Buoyed up by this affirmation, Nancy's husband began to take a look at some of his patterns. He was able to admit to her that he had never liked—in fact, he had hated—some of the dictatorial practices of his own father. And although as a boy he had sworn that when he grew up he would never treat others as he had been treated, he could see that he was doing exactly that. And as he hated it, so did his wife.

Nancy and her husband are a success story. I like success stories. That's why I told this one. Obviously, there are lots of examples of relationships that didn't make it. But Nancy and her husband succeeded because the healthier each became as an individual, the healthier their relationship became. Relationships cannot be healthier than the people involved.

Who You Are in a Relationship with Says as Much About You as It Does About the Other Person

Personally, I've always found this principle extremely irritating. If a relationship fails, we tend to look at our partner and wonder what's wrong with that person. We are so certain that if only he or she would change, our relationships could start to heal.

The fact is, as we have already stressed, who we end up in a relationship with is no accident. We may not know the reason, but the habits and patterns we have been practicing all our lives determine what sort of person fits our needs. As surely as night follows day, we will find someone "just right" for us. What "just right" means, of course, is what we have become used to, not necessarily what is healthy.

Reflecting on a marriage that had long ago broken up, a friend of mine once told me that his wife was "just my kind of woman, blond and passive." She was "just right," of course, but the marriage ended in divorce six months after it had begun, and the fear of that happening again had paralyzed the man. He says that he wants a permanent, committed, exclusive relationship, but he has never remarried. He still blames the woman who was "just right" for his paralysis. For him, there will never be a shortage of available women who are "just right." What he has to question, however, is what in him makes that kind of woman *his* kind.

The same is true for women who habitually find themselves in relationships with abusive men. There is not and never will be a shortage of abusive men around. The question is not about them but about what is going on in me that makes me vulnerable to that kind of person. This is not to say, of course, that there is ever any justification for abuse. But a woman who continually finds herself in abusive relationships can learn to understand herself and take the steps needed to change and protect herself from being a victim again.

The *other person* is not the primary issue in a relationship. The primary issue is always *me*. What is it about me, what pattern am I continuing to live out—probably unchallenged, possibly unnoticed—that draws me to this person and this relationship as powerfully and mindlessly as lemmings rush into the sea?

In relationships, my lot in life changes not when I first demand change of the other, but when I seriously take stock of myself.

Wherever You Go, There You Are

None of us can outperform our self-image. We became who we are when our habits and patterns formed our self-perception and our understanding of what is and isn't acceptable. As we see ourselves, we pick our partners—wherever we are. Geography will not change that fact. We can move anywhere on earth we want, and it will have no effect on the nature of our relationships. What we take with us when we move is ourselves and our self-image.

An example I often use to illustrate this principle is the simple observation that a Caretaker will marry a Baby every time.[1] Habits create needs, and Caretakers need Babies. Their self-esteem is based on taking care of and presumably saving someone who's in great need. Babies are only too glad to go along for the ride.

But at some point Caretakers usually get tired of taking care of Babies; they tend to resent what they've created. But if a Minnesota Caretaker, disgusted with Minnesota Babies, decides to go to Florida, who will he or she find there? Florida Babies, of course. And if he or she doesn't change and later takes off for New York, guess what? New York Babies. Same person, different place.

It may not seem that way at first, however. People get fooled in the early stages of a relationship. They need "Peacock Protection." At the outset of a relationship, both people are on their best behavior. All the signs of nurturing and caring are there: compliments, cards, the willingness to freely share feelings and ideas. But after all the preening of feathers and the strutting around has taken place, off comes the peacock suit and there is a turkey. Fooled again. The question is, how do you get Peacock Protection?

The only protection I know of is to take care of our own blindness. We cannot see in another what we are blind to in ourselves. To the extent that we are blind to ourselves as Caretakers or People-Pleasers, we are blind to our partners as Babies or Abusers. To the degree that we are blind to the effects of growing up in a less-than-perfect home, we are blind to the true character of others who grew up in similar backgrounds.

Moving doesn't help, not in the long run and not if you leave by yourself and go with a partner of many years. The fact is that whether you are alone or in a relationship, wherever you go, there you are.

If Nothing Changes, Nothing Changes

If the third principle is true, then the fourth principle is obvious. If moving doesn't help, then something has to change. Since we have no control over the choices that others make, the only option left is to take responsibility for ourselves. And that can be terribly risky. Nancy, for example, had no guarantee that her husband would prove pliable and be willing to grow. Since her growth meant change, the more she changed, the further she moved away from him. He could have just as easily dug in and said, "I'm not the one who's changed. You're the one who's different." And he would have been right; she was. He could have said, "I have been fine for you for years. Are you telling me that all of a sudden I'm not good enough?" What Nancy had to do was tell him that he was *not* just fine all those years, but neither was she. She did tell him and, happily, he gradually became willing to listen.

The point is, something must change. There are no guarantees what that will be. Some of the changes may come to be painful— so painful, in fact, that had we known how painful they would be at the outset, we never would have begun the journey at all. But now we have begun, now we know the difference; and we can never go back to the way it was.

The changes we make, whether they're painful or not, are made consciously and deliberately. No longer do things happen because that's the way it always was. No longer do we do what we do because we don't know how or have the strength to do anything else. Painful or not, we make decisions; and the change that follows is always better than powerless submission to forces we don't understand.

Consequences

These four principles show that there are reasons why we are in the relationships we're in, why we are still here, why the good ones are good and the failing ones fail. Based on these principles, let's now move on to the natural conclusion: the law of consequences.

All our behavior, whether or not we learned it in a dysfunctional home, has consequences. And the consequences don't depend on whether or not the situation we found ourselves in was fair, or whether we had enough knowledge, let alone wisdom, to handle it. Our decisions have consequences, often long-lasting ones. Here are some examples.

Withholding Nurturing

Nearly every man I have ever shared deeply with in my life has said, "We never shared feelings in our house. It was not allowed." If this is true of you, you may never have learned the ability to share feelings or offer nurturing in any number of important ways. You may find it difficult to be vulnerable or to ask for what you need. It may be hard to even offer sympathy or comfort when someone you care about is in pain. After all, you have been told, "Get tough, don't be a sissy." And it's no excuse to say, "You don't understand, I'm German (or Irish or Scandinavian or Polish)." It doesn't matter what nationality you are. What matters is what habits and patterns you grew up with.

Whatever the reasons, if you don't or aren't willing to learn to nurture your partner, he or she will develop emotional anemia and become spiritually hungry. Since hunger hurts and pain has a very loud voice, the more deprived your partner feels (and a deprived partner won't care if you're German or Polish or Martian, either), the more vulnerable your relationship is. Relationships are about nurturing; they're about finding a place in this frightening and often uncooperative world that is safe, a place where we are special and will be treated as such. That special treatment—which is at the core of the commitment we make in a primary relationship—is nurturing.

If a relationship doesn't have enough nurturing in it, the consequences can be severe. When those consequences strike, we tend to cry out about how unfair they are and to make new and radical promises about how different things are going to be from now on. But sometimes it's too late, and the relationship, like any other living thing, dies; when that happens, nothing can bring it back. Relationships die, as we will see later, from lack of trust. How can you ever trust a person who won't learn to nurture?

Think about the level of nurturing in your relationship. If the level is not enough, what might the consequences be? Are you willing to live with them?

Acting Out a Deep-rooted Fear of Abandonment

Most adults who were reared in dysfunctional homes develop an agonizing fear of abandonment, a sense that no matter how trustworthy their partners appear, sooner or later they will leave, in either the physical or the emotional sense of the word. Unless they are truly taking responsibility for their own recovery, such people can become so demanding and so dependent that they make it impossible for anyone to be in a loving relationship with them.

I have heard many men say something like this over the years:

"I'd love to do nice things for my partner, but I'm scared to. Giving her a gift is like spitting in the ocean. No matter what I do, it's not enough. If I do something once, it's demanded of me forever."

The result of not overcoming the fear of abandonment is that victims of this syndrome will not allow their partners to be present to them. They see their current partners as fresh embodiments of the person who betrayed them in the past. Yesterday's trauma is so powerful that it obliterates the present. The fear of abandonment, in fact, is so intense that it actually causes what is most feared: The current partner becomes exhausted trying to prove his or her worth and gives up.

As with people who are unable or unwilling to learn to nurture, the reasons why people suffer this paralyzing fear are obvious enough. They fear abandonment in the future because they have been abandoned and betrayed in the past, often in the most gruesome and pathetic manner. Understandable or not, this fear, if it's not dealt with, has consequences that are very real. The victims cause the loneliness they dread.

Not Giving Your Partner Sufficient Priority

It's reasonable to expect, when we enter a primary relationship, that our partner will assign us a high priority—that we will count in a big way. When this expectation is not realized, a disaster is set in motion and, sooner or later, the consequences will be felt.

The only proof of belief is behavior. Declaring that your partner is number one is not enough if the declaration doesn't square with the facts about what people, activities, and interests you spend the most time, energy, and effort on. Do a quick check by comparing a list of your supposed priorities with your actual expenditures of time and effort. Often they don't match.

The final proof is where your partner perceives himself or herself on your list of priorities. I always ask couples where each fits into the other's top ten priorities. Often enough they don't see themselves in the top five or six; sometimes they don't even make the top ten.

Most often, women will list "work" as their male partner's top priority. After that often comes "sports," "friends," "TV," or "hobbies." Men often think that "children" occupy the top position on their female partners' lists. If not "children," then "friends" or, increasingly, "work." Whatever the makeup of the list, the fact remains that the consequences can be serious if partners don't think they count to each other. Nearly always what we most object to in the behavior of our partners is exactly the behavior they object to in us. We resent having done to us what the other perceives we are doing in return.

Not Matching Actions with Words

A contradiction between words and actions is always serious, wherever it occurs. It's especially chaotic in the singles world, where the words say "no commitment, no strings attached" but the actions say the opposite. When two people become involved in an emotional, sexual relationship, regardless of the words spoken, one of them will come to expect an exclusive, committed relationship. After all, if it looks like a duck, walks like a duck, and quacks like a duck, it is reasonable to expect that it is a duck.

The person who finds himself or herself falling in love—all the while hearing and apparently accepting the words of noncommitment—may be in store for a massive heartache and may eventually have to live with the consequences of not having made a stand when the contradiction becomes apparent. That heartache can last a long time.

The other person in the relationship, who often claims innocence ("I was straight with you all along"), does not escape unharmed either. Withdrawal symptoms and a certain amount of agony accompany the tension of breaking up; and since commitment is not this person's long suit, he or she may decide that the best way to handle the mess is to leap into another noncommitted/committed relationship, even before the first one is over. So chaos is added to chaos and stress is layered upon stress.

Perhaps the worst consequence to befall a person who can't or won't make a commitment, however, is the loss of the ability to believe that anyone, ever, *can* make such a commitment! Sooner or later, people like this are bound to find someone they become serious about, but the ghosts and demons of the past will devilishly haunt their hearts. They and their partners will pledge fidelity, but doubts will remain; they can never be sure if their trust will be honored. They can only see others in the mirror of themselves, and that mirror can never reflect what was never put before it.

Not Talking Straight

The single most common reason for a failed relationship is not talking straight. For countless, understandable, sometimes tragic reasons, two people may not be able to tell each other how they feel, what they need, how something affects them. But as Nancy's exploding volcano shows, silence does not mean the absence of strongly felt emotions.

If we are not able to ask for what we need, chances are we will not get it. When we don't get what we need, we experience hurt; and hurt leads to anger. And when we're angry, we get even. Always! The method we use may be indirect, but it's real. Some otherwise uncreative people exhibit near genius at creating ways to get even.

It's clear that the dishonesty that accompanies "stuffing emotions" always leads to depression. This is the reason, I believe, that women suffer more depression than men. Society gives men the permission to be angry. Not so women. Rather than get angry, women get hurt. But it's impossible to be hurt without also being angry. When I'm working with a depressed woman, I always ask if she's angry about anything, and often enough she says no. But when I ask if her feelings ever get hurt, she often explodes: "Let me tell you the ways! Everyone I know hurts my feelings."

Not only does the individual suffer from such suppression, but so does the relationship. Not talking straight robs the participants of the opportunity to be present to one another in meaningful ways. It is easy enough to assume that a partner is unconcerned, but often he or she has never had the chance to *be* concerned. When counseling pries loose this fact, people are often astonished to learn that their partners are willing to do their best to open up to each other, if only they could learn what is being asked of them and could believe that they will be given the same gift in return.

The consequences of not talking straight range from ulcers and the risk of being sandbagged from behind all the way to never knowing that your best friend is sitting across from you at the breakfast table every day.

Having Affairs

There are endless ways to justify affairs. If we work hard enough at spinning out delusions, we can even arrive at the point where we convince ourselves that an affair is the proper—perhaps even the holy—thing to do.

Affairs siphon off energy and eliminate any chance that a relationship can work; sooner or later confusion and chaos seep into life, because words and actions never match. Affairs require sneaking and lying, and the deceit involved always leads to a loss of integrity accompanied by a corresponding loss of self-esteem. And the consequence of that guilt is the erosion of trust.

It's important to note that not all affairs have to be physical. Emotional affairs, which can be conducted without any sexual contact, are just as devastating. In an emotional affair I allow myself to become the center of your life, and you occupy the same place in mine. Our words may never acknowledge this fact, but every other means of communication assents: our tone of voice, the look in our eyes, the prearranged meetings at the water cooler, or the "accidental" meetings at a restaurant. We know very well what is going on, but our delusions allow it to continue.

We're especially vulnerable to emotional affairs with therapists, clergy, bosses, or coworkers. The special dilemma here is that we often go to these sorts of people when we need help in our lives and want to move forward. Instead, our emotional affairs with them are like invisible anchors that hold us fast to this place and time and prevent our growth.

Lonely, unhappy, searching people often fall prey to affairs. People who have been hurt or are terribly disillusioned are also vulnerable. Their stories can break your heart, but it doesn't matter. Affairs have consequences; and while the consequences may not kill you or have anything to do with a person being "good" or "bad," they do bring on the damage caused by pain and suffering.

Just as each of these behaviors has a negative consequence if it is acted out, so there is an equally strong positive consequence if it isn't acted out. Every decision no is also a decision yes. When we choose to nurture, we become more loving. When we overcome our deeply rooted fear of abandonment, we prove to ourselves that we are masters of our fate. When we let our partners know that they are top priority, we are likely to find that the gift is returned in full. When our behavior matches our words, our world is full of harmony and serenity. When we talk straight, we learn to trust in trust and we become people who can trust. When we refrain from having affairs of any kind, we create sane boundaries in our lives and give ourselves reason to like ourselves very much.

Reasons can be found for whatever happens in our relationships. When we know these reasons, we can make a good thing better and find our way out of a situation that may not be so healthy. *And* keep from going back, ever.

"We Are Ready!"

If all of this sounds like a lot of work, you're right. Sane relationships take a lot of work. For one thing, most of us were never taught the necessary skills. For another, like shoveling a ton of rocks, it's naturally hard work, even if we have the skills. In other areas of life—in business, school, sports—we accept the need to work hard to develop our skills. We need to have the same attitude about Stage II relationships.

Some years ago, on an airplane, I found myself talking to the assistant coach of a college football team bound for the Rose Bowl. Needless to say, the coaches and players had committed themselves to winning. They had viewed films of the opposing team, and had examined every play that team had executed in every game that year. Then they went back over each play and scrutinized every player at every position of every game that season. Countless hours went into that effort; and as a result every player knew what the player opposite him would do in any situation and what that player's strengths and weaknesses were.

It amazed me that this sort of preparation and effort would be spent on a game that only the people involved would remember. This young coach, his eyes sparkling (there was no question that the game was his top priority), repeatedly said, "Man, are we ready!" And they were. They won the Rose Bowl.

Long-gone football games and forever relationships. Preparation and effort. It makes you wonder.

Chapter 2

PERSONAL RELATIONSHIPS ARE
ABOUT LOVING

Primary personal relationships are about loving. Making love work is the goal of relationships.

If ever there was a topic on which you could gather lots of opinions it would be love. For some, love is a decision, cold and clear. For others, it is a feeling; if the feeling is not there, neither is love. For still others, it is a mystical experience of union and fulfillment.

The hard, cold fact is that no matter what love means to your partner, if he or she does not *experience* that love the relationship is in trouble. We can have widely different concepts about what food tastes good, but there is no question about whether or not a person is starving.

For years I've seen people in clinical situations trying to build or rebuild relationships without knowing the key factor: what their partners are asking of them. If I am to be present to another person in a meaningful way, I absolutely need to know what that person considers important emotional and spiritual food. Without this knowledge, working on our relationship is like being in a boxing ring with a world champion—and being blindfolded. Unlike the football coach who was more than ready for the Rose Bowl game, we're often *not* ready to deal with something as important as our relationships.

If I were to ask you to write down your partner's three most important needs or requests, what would they be? Try it. Then check with your partner to see if you're correct.

I frequently ask people in my seminars or in private counseling sessions to do this exercise. Are you surprised that their responses are wide of the mark, sometimes so wide that they don't even get one right? Yet if we are so much in the dark about the felt needs of our mates, how can we be present to them? As we will soon discuss, building trust with others requires being present to them in ways that are *significant to them*. And trust is the central issue in all relationships.

Three Questions

The people I work with find it extremely helpful to get firm, concrete answers from their partners to these three questions:

1. What does it *mean* to you to be loved?
2. What does it *take* for you to feel loved?
3. What are you *asking* of me in this regard?

Each answer yields information that is essential for building a healthy Stage II relationship.

What Does It Mean to You to Be Loved?

When you ask your partner this question, you ask, "What are your values, perceptions, and dreams about what it means to *you* (given who you are and where you've come from) to be loved?" The answers that I've collected to this question fall into seven areas, which can be presented as a hierarchy depicting the frequency of response and charting a movement from the most basic requirement ("safety") all the way to the top ("feeling special").[2] Here's what my respondents tell me about these levels:

1. *Safe.* Feeling safe has to do with sensing a freedom from abuse. The minimal requirement is to sense that "I will not be hurt here."

2. *Defended*. Feeling defended means having the sense that "I am not alone against the world." This doesn't mean that your partner has to agree with you on everything; but it does mean that, agree or not, your partner won't turn against you or side with others in a disrespectful way.

3. *Supported*. Feeling supported means having the sense that your partner is offering you encouragement—not just coming to your side during the hard times, but helping you grow, dream, and become better than you already are, and in a noncompetitive way. Support means that you don't have to compete with your partner, but will assist each other to be all that you can.

4. *Belonging*. Belonging means being included, believing that you are important enough to your partner to feel that you're part of a team. This often has to do with the inner realities, the sense that you want your partner to admit you into his or her inner world where you can share dreams, feelings, thoughts, and hidden hurts without fear of ridicule or betrayal.

5. *Cared about*. Feeling cared about is the same as feeling nurtured, which means being told, through certain actions or events (all the way from the giving of inexpensive cards, to being held, to making affectionate love) that you occupy an important place in your partner's life.

6. *Accepted*. Feeling accepted, which people seem to place enormous value on, means not being prodded by your partner to be other than, different than, or better than you are. It is also understood that no one is perfect and that growth is always desirable, but this doesn't preclude the need to be accepted as who you are at this moment in time. Knowing that your partner is not disappointed or unhappy with who you are— and, in fact, prizes you—is a very powerful part of the experience of being loved.

7. *Special*. While the term "special" may seem nebulous, it has a very concrete meaning. Feeling special means being prized,

being treated the way anything precious in life would be treated. Although the analogy is often made to the way people treat pets, antique cars, china, household treasures, or anything of that sort of value, feeling special is given the highest rating in the hierarchy of the experience of being loved.

Graphically, here's how these seven levels can be depicted:

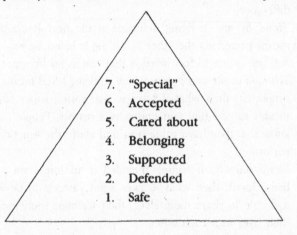

7. "Special"
6. Accepted
5. Cared about
4. Belonging
3. Supported
2. Defended
1. Safe

Of course, your graph may not look like this at all. But what does it look like? What does your partner's look like? If you don't know what your partner means when he or she experiences being loved, where is there to go?

What Does It Take for You to Feel Loved?

Once you know what love *means* to your partner as a practical, experiential matter, you are in a position to study this second question: What does it *take* from you for your partner to feel loved? You're not responsible for what your partner feels, and it's not necessary to need the same things your partner needs, of course. But it is important to know what is on your partner's list and in his or her heart, and you are responsible for doing everything in your power, short of sacrificing your integrity, to create an environment in which your partner can feel loved.

Building on the hierarchy of responses generated by the first question, we can see how respondents answered the second one.

1. *Don't abuse me.* If being safe represents the minimal level of being loved, then what it takes is to be free not only from physical abuse, but from the verbal and emotional abuse created by such dishonest patterns as blaming, alibis, and indifference.

2. *Stand by me.* If being defended is the next level, then it means perceiving the other as willing to stand by you. What it takes for me to feel loved is that you stand by me.

3. *Tell me I count as a person to you.* If being loved means being supported, then what it takes is that your partner communicates to you that you count as a person. People need to know that they have value over and above the function they perform.

4. *Share yourself.* If feeling included is an important part of being loved, then what it takes is for partners to be willing and able to share themselves, their feelings, their thoughts, their lives with each other.

5. *Be willing to go beyond your comfort zone.* To create an atmosphere where the partner feels cared about requires a willingness to move beyond just what is comfortable or what you are inclined to do.

6. *Provide hospitality.* If acceptance is important, then hospitality is how it is put into practice. Hospitality encourages a sense that you're welcome, that your hosts are glad you've come to visit. At the heart of every runaway, every failed relationship, every divorce is a lack of hospitality, the feeling that "you don't care about me." On the other hand, every healthy relationship radiates the opposite: a sense that hospitality is a priority, that someone cares about you.

7. *Surrender.* To surrender in a relationship means not to give up but to deliberately remain within the boundaries of what you've chosen, to remain faithful to your commitment to your

partner. Even if an opportunity for another relationship arises, you say no—not because you're afraid of being caught, but because you choose not to for the sake of the good you have chosen. Surrender gives serenity to your fidelity.

Graphically, here is how this list would look:

7. Surrender
6. Provide hospitality
5. Move beyond
   comfort zone
4. Share yourself
3. Tell me I count
2. Stand by me
1. Don't abuse me

When you put these lists side by side, you can see a causal relationship.

What the practical experience of being loved means to me	What it takes for the experience of being loved to be created for me
7. Special	7. Surrender
6. Accepted	6. Provide hospitality
5. Cared about	5. Move beyond comfort zone
4. Belonging	4. Share yourself
3. Supported	3. Tell me I count
2. Defended	2. Stand by me
1. Safe	1. Don't abuse me

What does your hierarchy look like? Although you may not know at first, the information is very important.

Means	Takes
7.	7.
6.	6.
5.	5.
4.	4.
3.	3.
2.	2.
1.	1.

Knowing, of course, does not mean doing. You may well decide that what your partner tells you is silly and unreasonable, and that you're not going to react or respond to it. But at least you would be making your decision not to participate from an informed point of view. The opposite hope is that information like this arms you with something that gives you a realistic chance to make decisions that will improve your relationship. That hope is reasonable and legitimate, because the information it is based on is so pertinent to relationships: our partner's experience of being loved.

What Are You Asking of Me?

In response to learning what being loved means to your partner, the next question has to be, "What are you asking of me?" This third question puts teeth in the whole process by getting down to specific behavior. A response like "respect me" or "let me know you care" is too general to be of any use. What's needed is a list of concrete actions.

The technique I use to elicit this information is a sentence-completion exercise. Each person needs to write down (not just think about) two or three responses to each of the following statements:

1. When you _____, I feel most loved (or cared about, safe, etc.)

Again, the most important part of the task is to be as specific as possible. Here are some responses:

- "call me just to see how I'm doing"
- "tell me you love me"
- "ask my opinion before you make up your mind"

2. When you _____, I feel most discounted (or used, taken advantage of, etc.)

Again, fill in whatever best indicates what contributes to the worst feeling in your relationship and what you should stop doing. Here are some examples:

- "criticize me about the way I look every day"
- "bounce checks"
- "are consistently late for everything we do"

Now, fill in your responses to these two questions:

1. What I ask of you:

2. What I ask you not to do:

The information this exercise provides is not to be used as black-mail, nor should it be used to take your partner hostage. These propositions are requests for you to do what it takes to create an experience of trust, safety, and love. As long as your partner's requests don't violate your integrity, you should listen to them intently and take them seriously. The pathway to growth in your relationship is now clear. *Do what counts to your partner* and *stop doing what discounts your partner*.

The last thing to do is process the information that this exercise yields. Run what you learn from both questions through this checklist:

- *Do I clearly understand* (not necessarily agree to) what my partner is asking of me?
- *Is what my partner asks reasonable?* A request to "always make me feel good" is unreasonable since no one can make anyone *always* feel anything. Likewise, a request to "never abandon me" puts all the burden on you, when in fact, because of what happened in your partner's family of origin, he or she may continue to feel abandoned no matter what you do or do not do. Besides, since no one is perfect, perfection (as in, "always do this or that") is an unreasonable request.
- *Can I do it?* It's important to know whether you have the skill that your partner is asking you to use. If you don't, you'll fail, and that failure will set off a series of reactions that will further worsen your relationship.
- *Am I willing?* Maybe you're able, but you're not willing. That doesn't necessarily make you a terrible person, but it needs to be stated clearly. If you're not willing to do what your partner thinks is necessary, you should both know it in advance so that later, possibly painful decisions aren't shrouded in confusion. Being willing also means being willing to develop a skill you don't currently possess (like sharing your feelings, talking straight, taking responsibility for your own growth). Are you willing to say, "I can't do this now, but I'll try to learn how"?

- *What changes do I need to make?* If you are willing but not able, be clear about what you're committing yourself to. Under pressure or in a moment of passion (or both), you may commit yourself to making changes without considering the effort the changes will require. Later on, there may be resentment when you become aware of the price. But if you buy it, so to speak, don't complain when the bill comes later.

- *Will your partner reciprocate?* If *you* are willing and able, is your partner? This is important. If your partner won't spend the same amount of energy and risk the same vulnerability, you're setting yourselves up for a lose-lose situation.

The Anatomy of a Relationship

The more clearly you understand the anatomy of a relationship, the more important what you learn through these exercises becomes. Although relationships are built on subjective experiences, they still have rules; and just as we would hate to have a surgeon operate on us who had no knowledge of human anatomy, it is also fatal to start work on a relationship without knowing the basics.

Recently, while I was jogging on the upper track at a health club, I happened to notice a tennis lesson in progress on the floor below. A tennis pro, with infinite patience, was instructing a novice. He would lob the ball gently over the net, encouraging the sweating newcomer to keep his eye on the ball and "just swing level." The student returned maybe one in five balls.

What struck me about this lesson was how much it could teach us about relationships. In a relationship, we are totally dependent on the willingness and ability of our partner to play fair. No matter how marvelous one player may be, if the other player is not able or willing to play, there won't be a game. The point is *the game*, not one person's level of skill.

As I trudged on, I began to imagine variations on this tennis theme, and I began to match up these variations with different clients I have worked with. One version involves a fairly skilled player who's got new shoes, a newly strung racket, and a new can of balls. He's ready and he desperately wants a stimulating game, but his partner is sitting on the bench, reading a newspaper, unconcerned. No matter how badly he wants to play, there won't be a game.

In another version, sportsmanship has been thrown out the window; winning is all that counts, and if that means cheating, so be it. If it means playing psychological games on your opponent or trying to intimidate him, then look out. Here, as in some relationships, "opponent" is exactly the right word, isn't it? However it's defined, winning is what counts in this kind of relationship, not nurturing, companionship, or helping one another. Opponents swing away with frightening force, and at the end of the game each exhausted partner staggers off, proclaiming victory.

In still another version, neither player will play. They don't even know what got them to the court in the first place, but there they are, half-heartedly swinging away. It's a boring game.

If your relationship was a tennis match, what would it look like? To help fill in the picture, let's use the context of a tennis match to examine five words: both, trust, trustworthy, growth, program.

Both

A relationship cannot be healthier than *both* people are willing and able to make it. We can look at this word in three ways.

- *Want.* Your partner on the other side of the net may not want the same sort of relationship you do. You may want the caring, sharing, coresponsible kind; your partner may want to be either a hermit or a tyrant, or may even see the relationship as a motel—a place to eat and sleep. If you and your partner (or your children, for that matter) don't want the same kind of game, there can be nothing but confusion and hurt.
- *Willing.* If what it takes to make a relationship work is for you to join a Twelve-Step program, would you be willing to do so? If you and your partner decided that you had to set aside time

each week for dialogue, would the willingness be there? If you decided that you needed to take the time to get to know each other all over again, would you be willing to make the effort? If we feel that the hunger for the intimacy only healthy relationships provide is the most important quest of life, are we willing to do what it takes to make the quest a reality? We may dearly want to play a marvelous game of tennis, but we both must be willing to put in the effort it takes to do so.

- *Able.* Good will, however, is not enough. Healthy relationships, as I've stressed, take skills that can be learned. And if both partners want the same kind of game and are willing to learn the skills necessary, there's no limit to the quality of the game we can enjoy.

Trust

The second of our five words is *trust.* The quality of any relationship is determined by the degree of trust present. What is not so obvious is that trust means more than sexual fidelity or financial honesty. Trust demands both of these, of course, but it also means being able to count on the other person to play fair—to hit the ball back when you knock it over the net. Trust means that you'll be each other's best cheerleader and that you'll be present to each other in ways that *are* important—not just ways you assume are important. (The exercises presented earlier in this chapter are essential to developing trust.) Trust depends on communication. If there is sufficient trust, a couple can communicate about anything—even if they don't agree—because each partner will be respectfully heard and taken seriously.

Trustworthy

The only way you can generate trust is to be trustworthy. To strengthen your relationship you have to ask not, "Can I trust my partner?" but, "Can my partner trust me?" The first movement has to be back toward ourselves, not toward them. We need to ask ourselves, "Where do I need to grow to be a more trustworthy partner?"

Of course, if the couple is having a rough go of it, that's the last question either partner wants to hear. More often the agenda is to get into counseling so that the *other* person can get some help, accompanied by the unspoken sentiment, "and God knows she or he needs it."

But pointing at the other person and demanding change is not where progress begins. What does happen is that one person digs in his or her heels and says, "I won't change until you do." When that happens, they retreat to their separate barricades and start throwing bombs at one another.

Only when the partners are willing to look at themselves and take responsibility for their own personal growth and change will progress be made. And this is a commitment they *both* need to make; if they don't, one is left paying the bill. Do you trust people who won't pay their bills?

My wife is one of the world's great celebrators. She finds joy in just about anything—from a grand vacation to ants walking across the cake at a picnic. I, on the other hand, tend to be a worrier. I believe that if anything can go wrong, it certainly may go wrong. So we have to be on guard.

Imagine the risk of a celebrator marrying a worrier. If I am not willing first of all to stand back and examine myself, how can I expect my wife to do the same? And it is precisely my own blind spot about myself that makes me untrustworthy. The less trustworthy I am, the less trust I promote in our relationship. And since trust is the name of the game, I had better be concerned about it!

Here's an example. A few years ago, my wife won a trip to New York. She was typically ecstatic, both because she had never been to New York and because I was to be included in the trip. We followed our usual pattern. My wife joyfully prepared for the trip, while I began to describe in detail all the disasters that could befall us. Fed up, my wife finally announced one day that I was no longer invited. "You're ruining my trip already," I was told. "You are fussing and moping around, so I think it would be better if you just stayed home. You can be unhappy here just as well as in New York."

"But I want to go," I protested.

"Then deal with your stinking attitude," she told me. "Either change it or stay home."

You can see that I wasn't playing fair. The old, destructive, learned behavior was in control. By not playing fair, I was not trustworthy, and trust was taking a beating.

So I shaped up, we went, and had a marvelous time.

The fact is, no matter what our upbringing was like, no matter who our family of origin is, no matter what self-destructive patterns we learned in the past, *we are responsible*. We can take control of our lives. We can embark on the path of Stage II recovery and become people capable of enjoying Stage II relationships.

A counselor friend of mine, who works exclusively with battered women, told me that her clients constantly ask, "Are there any good men out there?" Although very conscious of their situation, she responds, "Are there any good women in here?" She knows all too well the tendency to point a finger outward and find problems out there. And she knows that the only way the women she counsels will recover and find healthy relationships is to start by looking within. In her view, it is no accident that they ended up in relationships with abusive men in the first place. If whatever perceptions that got them involved in abusive relationships in the first place don't change, she sadly knows that she will see these women again.

Growth

Our fourth word is *growth*. Growth means change; people do not become more trustworthy by accident. It takes a deliberate, conscious effort. One of my central principles—if nothing changes, nothing changes—is never more true than when we're considering personal growth, especially in the context of relationships. Something has to be different if the quality of our relationships is to improve. Since we have no control over the other person, we can only demand change of ourselves.

In later chapters, we will take a specific look at some possible areas that may demand change if we are to become more trustworthy and generate more trust, which will allow both partners to develop a dynamic game.

Program

The fifth word of our explanation is *program*. Just as we do not become more trustworthy by accident, neither do we grow. It takes a program, which is but another word for practice. Through practice we learn the skills necessary to do anything, whether it's to build a healthy relationship or improve our serve. The particulars of working a program will be dealt with later.

The following picture shows how these five words fit together, flow together, and feed one another. See if you can explain the process to yourself and then test your grasp of the concepts by explaining them to your partner.

If—

Both participants want, are willing, and work at developing the skills necessary, then

Trust is generated between the two because both have proven themselves

Trustworthy by playing fair. The process of becoming trustworthy is the result of working for

Growth, which, in turn, is the result of working an intelligent State II *Program.*

The more *both* people are working their *program,* the more *trust* is generated because both are then increasingly *trustworthy*—and that takes us back to *both*.

Skills

If relationships require skills, what might these skills be? Allow me to suggest six: two sets of three skills each. And since nothing is real unless it is personal, I would ask you, as you read about each skill, to rate yourself and your partner (or your children or your parents or someone you're in a relationship with) on each skill. Assign a number from 1 (no skill) to 10 (perfect skill) for each of the six.

If your scores are low, you'll need to be realistic about what's possible; but know that people can change, and new skills can be learned. Relationships that are on the ropes can be turned around and made gloriously beautiful if you're willing to work at it.

1. Knowing What You Really Need

This may sound simple, but it isn't. Caretakers need, or think they need, more people to take care of. Martyrs feel they need more pain. Workaholics sense they need more work. Perfectionists think they need more time to get more done and more talent to do it better. There are also those among us who have lived so long and practiced so hard at wanting nothing, that they have destroyed their sense of needing anything.

It may well be that what we truly need to become more human, more whole, more holy is simply a hug. Maybe what we need is not more work but more time off. Maybe what we truly need is not to do without but to order ourselves a feast.

Sometimes what we really need is not to be a pillar of iron but to surrender ourselves and allow our weakness and vulnerability to show through. Maybe what we need is to let others take care of us for a change.

Obviously, the options and possibilities can vary greatly. The point is that if we are not in touch with our needs or willing to get in touch with them, we cannot ask another person to be present to us. If we don't talk straight about our needs, chances are they will never be met; and if they're not, the result will be anger, which always leads to attempts to get even.

Rate yourself and your partner from 1 to 10.

2. Asking to Have Your Needs Met

Once you've identified your needs, the next task is to share them. There's no substitute for straight talk. Even if your partner does not listen honestly after you have talked straight, you have the satisfaction and self-esteem that come from playing honestly yourself.

Many people give themselves an 8 or a 9 on this skill, but the proof is in the behavior. When was the last time you actually shared a need with your partner? If your answer is 1975, maybe your score is inflated.

Asking for what we need is terribly difficult for many of us. It runs contrary to the stern rules we learned in our past. Under the banner of strength or virtue, we deny giving a significant person in our life the pleasure of getting us something that we value.

Asking for what we need does not mean blackmailing our partners or *demanding* that they give us something. What it means is patiently, clearly leveling with another person, communicating a need that is essential to the birth of trust.

Rate yourself and your partner from 1 to 10.

3. Creating an Environment in Which Your Partner Knows You Care About His or Her Needs

Notice that I did not say that you should take responsibility for your partner's needs; that's dependent caretaking. Rather, because we care and love, we create an environment where the other person knows we care.

A woman I know, a recovering adult child of a dysfunctional home who was severely denied nurturing in her youth, recently told me a touching story. This woman is divorced and has a young daughter. Because she is recovering, she is working hard to be attuned to the feelings and needs of her daughter, who misses her father and sometimes feels lonely and lost. The mother has to work all day to make ends meet, so the little girl often feels neglected.

Eventually, the daughter was able to convey her feelings to her mother, who decided to form a "love club." She took time off from work and the three of them—mother, daughter, and teddy bear—went on a picnic. The little girl's love pot got filled, and sunshine was everywhere. Why would we trust anyone who doesn't care about our needs?

A man told me about something he did for his wife, a totally committed Irishwoman whose favorite day of the year is St. Patrick's Day. He could care less about that holiday, but he does care about his wife and the quality of their relationship. So this year he found a store that sold cardboard Irish figures strung along eight-foot-long string, and he pasted the figures over the archway that led into their kitchen. When his wife came home she was ecstatic, not only for the touch of the green, but because of the obvious concern her husband had shown in noticing what she valued and doing what counted to her.

Creating this trusting environment does not mean that what's important to your partner has to be important to you. The real issue is not picnics and teddy bears and Irish figures at all, of course; it's creating an environment where the other person knows you care. It is about getting out of your comfort zone sufficiently to make room for the other.

Rate yourself and your partner from 1 to 10.

4. Knowing What You Feel

This sounds simple enough. Everybody knows what they feel. But do they?

What we feel is what we practice. What we feel is usually what we have been given permission to feel. If we grew up being told that we "shouldn't feel that way," we learned that whatever "that way" was was not acceptable. And we never learned to understand or expand our vocabulary of feelings.

We can't share feelings we don't have, and unless we know what we feel we can't share our feelings.

One marvelous man I know has been sober two years and is truly into Stage II recovery. He came to know that the menu of feelings he is in touch with wouldn't fill a postage stamp. So he devised an ingenious plan to change that; we could all learn from what he did.

Somewhere along the way he got hold of a list of about 150 feelings. He put that list in a clear plastic folder, which sits on the front seat of the car he's often in as a salesman. Whenever he is stuck in traffic or stalled at a red light, he picks up his folder and goes to work. He reads the names of feelings off the list—*sympathy, anger, joy, despair*—and asks himself if he is really familiar with each one. He thinks about situations in which he might experience such a feeling. In short, he practices. He is a hero. He is making Stage II decisions about his life.

How clear are you about the difference between hurt and anger? Do you know when you are feeling fearful and when that fear turns to rage? Do you know the difference between feeling guilty and feeling sad?

Rate yourself and your partner from 1 to 10.

5. Sharing Your Feelings

We may eventually develop a complete vocabulary of our feelings; but unless we share them with another, we will always remain strangers. Through sharing, we create the closeness and intimacy that we so desperately seek in our relationships. Conversely, we can share anything else—our homes, our bodies, our meals, our money—and if we don't accompany it with feelings, we won't be close.

Sometimes we don't know how we feel. But instead of saying, "I'm not sure. Give me some time to process my feelings and I'll tell you when I can," we often say, "Fine. I feel fine." Smoke may be coming out of our ears, or we may be so sad that we're shedding invisible—or even real—tears, or we may be so scared that our knees are shaking; but we still say, "Okay. I'm fine. How are you?"

It is difficult to trust someone who will not or cannot share feelings. But if we want to badly enough, we can always learn, regardless of all the reasons we can muster not to and regardless of our previous inexperience. How can you not trust someone who is obviously working hard to develop a skill necessary for a relationship?

Rate yourself and your partner from 1 to 10.

6. Creating an Environment in Which Your Partner Knows You Care About His or Her Feelings

Again, this doesn't mean taking responsibility for your partner's feelings, but making a mighty effort to communicate that how and what your partner feels is important to you.

Do you compliment a partner who feels old on how nice he or she looks? Are you willing to celebrate with a partner who's wildly happy? If a partner's worried about something, will you share the concern or merely run an old tape and say, "You shouldn't feel that way. Nothing to worry about. Stop being a baby."

In the past several years, much has been written about the phenomenon of so-called male menopause or midlife crisis. Whatever its name, it's certainly real for many men, and the reasons for it are easy enough to understand (if only men would start talking about it). At some point in their lives men start slowing down physically, their stomachs sag, and their hair starts to fall out. Chances are they are as advanced in their profession as they'll ever get; their bosses may look like their children. And unless they are in conscious contact with their feelings and are able to share them with their partners, men at this point become frightened, feel disjointed, and are often resentful that life is rushing by. The feeling that so much is yet to be done but never will be hangs like an anchor on their hearts. A sea of emotions often accompanies this midlife adjustment. Is it safe to talk about my fears and hurts? Will anyone listen? Will anyone try to understand?

Obviously, no one can make the decisions for a man or a woman stuck in a midlife crisis other than the person himself or herself. But we can be of enormous help by creating an environment where our partner knows that he or she is cared about.

Score yourself and your partner from 1 to 10.

Look at your scores. Is your score higher than your partner's? That's usually the case. It's also quite common for each partner in a couple to give himself or herself a high score and the partner a low score *for the same skill*, a situation that speaks volumes about the kind of job each has done communicating with the other.

People in relationships need skills, and you can learn skills if you want to badly enough. Even though we may have been robbed of the opportunity to learn these skills early in life, the truth is that we were all made for love: The deepest yearning in our hearts is for the connectedness that comes with healthy relationships. So, in a sense, each of us has a head start in our quest for that which we seek.

Heaven and Hell

Let me summarize all of these principles in a venerable Chinese parable.

A very old man knew that he was going to die very soon. Before he died, he wanted to know what heaven and hell were like, so he visited the wise man in his village.

"Can you please tell me what heaven and hell are like?" he asked the wise man.

"Come with me and I will show you," the wise man replied.

The two men walked down a long path until they came to a large house. The wise man took the old man inside, and there they found a large dining room with an enormous table covered with every kind of food imaginable. Around the table were many people, all thin and hungry, who were holding twelve-foot chopsticks. Every time they tried to feed themselves, the food fell off the chopsticks.

The old man said to the wise man, "Surely this must be hell. Will you now show me heaven?"

The wise man said, "Yes, come with me."

The two men left the house and walked farther down the path until they reached another large house. Again they found a large dining room and in it a table filled with all kinds of food. The people here were happy and appeared well fed, but they also held twelve-foot chopsticks.

"How can this be?" said the old man. "These people have twelve-foot chopsticks and yet they are happy and well fed."

The wise man replied, "In heaven the people feed each other."

Chapter 3

UNDERSTANDING YOURSELF: YOUR SIDE OF THE NET

A tennis match can only be as exciting and successful as the quality of the players allows. Although we can't control the ability or the attitude of the player on the other side of the net, we can control our own play by deciding who we want to play with and how much we want to exert ourselves to improve our game. It's this side of the net I want to concentrate on in this chapter.

Depending on the lessons we grew up with and the skills we possess, we may or may not believe that we can control our side of the net in our relationships with others. Many passive adults feel powerless over what happens in their relationships or even over who they are in relationships with. Some grow up believing, whether they are aware of it or not, that they have little or no freedom to decide whether to be in a healthy relationship—it's all "their" fault. "They" are to blame. We hook up with ducks and then bitterly complain because they aren't eagles. But a duck has the right to be a duck. The real issue is, if we wanted to fly with eagles, why are we choosing to be on the ground with the ducks? It's a *me* issue, not a *them* issue.

I often ask participants in my workshops if they've ever been in a failed relationship or in a relationship that repeatedly runs into trouble. Hands fly wildly.

Then I inform these people that we are going to take a multiple-choice test to determine why they think their relationships were troubled. I offer four options and ask each member of the workshop to vote for the one that best describes his or her reason:

1. *Because my partner was a jerk* is the first option, and it usually gets a lot of votes, especially when I encourage people to be honest with themselves.

2. *Bad luck* is another popular choice. Some people will always believe that no one is at fault, that it's just the luck of the draw. But, when questioned, most of these people will also agree that bad luck has followed them around all their lives. If the same luck befalls people wherever they go, maybe luck has nothing to do with it. Maybe it's something deeper, like option three.

3. *God's will*, the third option also has its followers. They decide that God predestined, for all eternity, that they would buy into the painful, destructive relationships they've endured. Some also believe that it's their lot in life to suffer, and be-cause of their sufferings—which God has willed—they will enjoy a higher place in heaven.

4. *Given who I am and who my partner is, there's no way it could be any different.* This option usually gets the biggest response, because people do tend to understand that it's the lessons of our past that drive our decisions today, not an ac-cident or the whim of a celestial being. How *could* it be any different, given who we are?

All of this points to the need to take a long, hard look at *me*. The more responsibility I take for who I am and what I do, the better my decisions will be. The better my decisions are, the health-ier my situation becomes. The healthier my situation is, the less inclined and less willing I will be to enter into an insane relation-ship again. The healthier I become, the better I feel about myself; and the better I feel about myself, the more I will do the things that work for me. In this context, it is totally correct to say "I can only change me, but I am everything."

Allow me to share a beautiful success story with you.

Years ago, a man of forty-five sought me out for help with an abuse problem. He had physically abused his first wife several times before his violence finally put her in the hospital. Successive relationships followed a similar course, and he was loaded with shame and guilt. As we worked through his family of origin, however, it became clear to him that he was repeating the patterns of his father.

"He kicked me so damn hard," the man told me, shaking with rage at the memory, "that my chin snapped up and I almost bit my tongue in two. I was fifteen. I turned to him, picked up a club, and told him if he ever laid a finger on me again I'd kill him." Although he hadn't talked with his father in thirty years, he had taken from his childhood all the machinery necessary to perpetuate a pattern of abuse: to do to others what he so terribly hated being done to himself.

After his third marriage had failed because of his abuse, he sought the affection he desperately needed through promiscuous sex and multiple relationships. He got a lot of sex, but he never got the affection and intimacy he needed. All his relationships were shot through with abuse of one kind or another, and the results were always the same: shame, guilt, self-hatred, and the uncontrollable urge to run—and keep on running—to even more sex and more work.

Finally, he had a child with one of the women he was involved with. This little boy is six years old. The man told me how he would take his son, when he was a tiny baby, and lay him on his stomach, holding him there the way he wished he'd been held. As he sat in my office, recounting these events, tears formed in his eyes. As much as anything they were the tears of tenderness. That close, intimate connection with his infant son had so touched and healed the wound within that the experience of that beauty was still strong.

Now, years later, he lives in the same city as his son and his son's mother, but they do not live together. This man no longer abuses women, he no longer is engaged in multiple relationships, and he spends every other week with his son. "Mostly," he says, "we just sit around and talk. We are close. He still remembers taking naps on my chest. I don't know what the feeling is, but it is better than any sex I ever experienced."

I hope this man is moving to the point where he can experience both sex *and* intimacy. They don't have to be mutually exclusive, even though they had been for him. For now, however, he knows what love is through the experience of his son. He is working his program as hard as he can, a day at a time, to widen his capacity to experience genuine intimacy. He is taking care of his side of the net and, as he does, his game gets better and better.

Habits

Before he had begun his family-of-origin work, this man had no idea that patterns were operating in his life. He hadn't seen the connection between his past, constantly practiced lessons and the present consequences of those lessons. As far as he was concerned, he had left his father behind—"buried him so deep he would never come back," as he said.

The father, of course, had not been buried at all. He not only still lived, but was fully in charge of what was going on. The abuse this man committed in the 1970s and 1980s was just a repetition of the abuse he had received thirty years earlier.

What we practice becomes habit.[3] Habits control the quality of our lives by dictating to us the options we see as possible. To successfully take care of our side of the net means we must recognize the habits in control of our lives and make appropriate and healthy decisions about them.

Rooted in our unconscious, habits are living things that are difficult to kill. They are not simply irritating behavioral ticks—like biting our nails or grinding our teeth. They are patterns of behavior that define for us, as individuals, what is "normal." Our habits control how we look at and relate to the world around us.

Six Patterns of Behavior

Let's take a look at six general patterns of codependent behavior. I don't intend to provide scientific definitions, nor do I wish to suggest that the patterns are mutually exclusive. Rather, they simply represent the ways that codependents respond to the world. The patterns are Caretaker, People-Pleaser, Martyr, Workaholic, Perfectionist, and Tap Dancer. Each pattern of response was learned in childhood and practiced for a lifetime, and they all create pain and discomfort throughout a person's life.

If you practice one or more of these patterns, it doesn't mean that you're bad. It simply means that these patterns were demanded if you were to get the "good stuff" (love, acceptance, self-esteem) when you were growing up. As you look at each pattern, see which ones best describe you.[4]

The Caretaker

Caretakers grew up learning and believing that they are good to the extent that they take responsibility for other people's happiness and success. A Caretaker's motto is, "I am responsible for all things and all people at all times." They're not just people who do nice things for others; in fact, they could do more of that. Caretakers pass over the line from being virtuous to being neurotic when they insist on doing for others what others should do and need to do for themselves. Because they take it upon themselves to make the essential decisions that others need to make to grow up.

Caretakers, also called enablers, are the worst enemies of people they love most; as long as someone else is taking care of them, they never have to take care of themselves.

Habits create needs. As we've already seen, Caretakers need Babies—people who grew up learning they didn't have to do anything for themselves. Of course they didn't have to—because someone was always around who would make sure they didn't.

If you are on your side of the net looking across with fire in your eyes at a person who is unwilling to make decisions or take responsibility, take a look at yourself first. Where did your partner learn that it was acceptable to act in such a manner? How long has he or she been able to get away with it? What will this person lose if he or she won't change?

All the answers, of course, lead back to your side of the net. Chances are your partner will feel no need to change until there's a reason to, and that reason will come from you. You're not responsible for your partner's change, but you *are* responsible for your own; and what you set in motion may make you both healthier, more skilled, and better able to share in a Stage II relationship.

TASK: Reflecting on the six skills necessary for a Stage II relationship (pages 49 to 54), think about how a Caretaker would meet these criteria. As you do, it will become clear how and why Caretakers have difficulty in relationships.

Here are some possible responses to this task, depending on how deeply a particular Caretaker is stuck in this pattern.

1. *Know what you really need.* Caretakers feel they need more people to take care of, so they find more dependent, broken, wounded people to surround themselves with. A Caretaker's ultimate goal, however, is not to heal these people but to feed their need to find someone to fix them. That's a role they gladly and automatically fill.

2. *Ask to have your needs met.* Caretakers never ask. Because they are too busy feeding the needs of others, they often feel used and unappreciated—which of course they are.

3. *Create an environment where your partner knows you care about his or her needs.* Instead, Caretakers create an atmosphere of dependency in the name of love. This is not to say that they don't love, but that because they lack the skills, the result of their effort is an unhealthy relationship in which love is blocked.

4. *Know what you feel.* Nonrecovering Caretakers are not generally in touch with many of their feelings. It has become

normal for them to discount any feelings that suggest that they are needy or need to be taken care of. So they aren't; and thus they are often angry, tired, jealous, or in a downright rage. Like Nancy, they are silent volcanoes, waiting to explode.

5. *Share your feelings.* Because they are not in touch with their feelings, Caretakers don't have any way of sharing them.

6. *Create an environment where your partner knows you care about his or her feelings.* A genuinely healing emotional environment demands that the individuals involved are aware enough to know what feelings and behaviors to support. What's normal for a Caretaker is to give in the name of love, to tolerate passivity in the name of caring, and to promote irresponsibility in the name of support.

Score yourself from 1 (not at all) to 10 (very much) according to how much you act out the role of Caretaker in any given relationship. Then write a paragraph in which you outline the consequences of this sort of behavior in a relationship.

The People-Pleaser

People-Pleasers have never learned to say no. If they say no, they think that others would get mad at them; and when that happens, it means they're bad people and would be abandoned by the people they love.

In order to avoid this fate, People-Pleasers learn to lie; emotional dishonesty becomes a way of life. When you ask People-Pleasers how they're doing, they invariably say "Fine," no matter how hurt, tired, lonely, or angry they are. When you ask them what they want to do, they say, "I don't care. Whatever you want," no matter how badly they want to do something. When you ask them if they have any objections to something that's planned for the future, they say, "If that's what you want, it's fine with me."

People-Pleasers have an all-consuming need to wear a white hat. No matter what it takes, they need to be the good guys. If that means overturning a household rule when a son or daughter pleads, they will do it in a second, even if it means betraying a promise made to their partners. (Their need to be thought well of by their children came first.) If it means staying in a toxic relationship with a partner while initiating a second relationship with someone else, they will, because they don't want to hurt their partner's feelings. If it means sacrificing their integrity by not telling the truth, they'll lie.

When they look across the net at their partners, People-Pleasers often see insensitive people. This is not surprising, since People-Pleasers seldom experience their needs being met. In fact, they frequently find themselves in abusive relationships. Why? People-Pleasers don't have their needs met because no one knows what they are. The fear of offending anyone overrides any thought that they may have needs or that they may count enough to have any importance. One People-Pleasing woman I know says that she smiles during the infrequent times she speaks of her pain at a support group; the smile is her way of saying, "This hurts, but it really isn't that important."

TASK: Reflecting on the six Stage II skills (pages 49 to 54), describe how a People-Pleaser would measure up. Score yourself from 1 (not at all) to 10 (very much) according to how much you act out the People-Pleaser pattern in any given relationship. Then write a paragraph in which you outline the consequences of this sort of behavior in a relationship.

The Martyr

Martyrs have learned a hard lesson: "If things are going well, watch out. Life is not meant to be too happy." The techniques they use to fulfill their prophecies of doom are ingenious. Worry is the best. It makes sure that today is not *too* good. When the upper limit of what Martyrs can stand in the way of happiness has been reached, they can always worry about war, taxes, famine, or pollution.

Guilt is another infuriating weapon. During a happy celebration, Martyrs will remind us of the starving children of Asia. When we buy a new dress or suit, Martyrs will think of those who only have gunny sacks to wear. Every time we're happy, Martyrs will give us the opportunity to share their worries.

Martyrs are terrified of pleasure. They feel they have no need or right to share in the truly good things life has to offer. And since a loving relationship is about the best there is in life, when a Martyr's relationship becomes too good, out come the weapons, and the satisfaction that love and intimacy bring about is brought down to an acceptable level.

It's particularly tempting for Martyrs to hide this pattern behind a religious veil. In the name of God's will or destiny or virtue, Martyrs embrace and cause hurt and pain. They are psychologically stuck at Good Friday. They remain on the cross, unable to move on to Easter Sunday with the God they often proclaim.

TASK: Reflecting on the six Stage II skills (pages 49 to 54), evaluate how a Martyr would measure up. Score yourself from 1 (not at all) to 10 (very much) according to how much you act out the role of the Martyr in any given relationship. Then write a paragraph in which you outline the consequences of this sort of behavior in a relationship.

The Workaholic

Workaholics take one of two forms. One kind is the driven person who is compulsively productive and professionally successful. The other kind never has much to do, but is always busy at it. This kind has learned that good people are never idle, even if it means being as busy as a beaver but as unproductive as an infant.

Whatever the form, the underlying belief is the same: Projects and productivity are more important than people. Workaholics often seem to act as if people were an inconvenience rather than a sacred necessity for healthy living. They rarely have much patience with or sympathy for the human faults and failings of others.

That doesn't mean that workaholics can't love. Like all human beings, they can. Many, in fact, loudly protest that all the work they're doing is but a sacrament of love for their families. But around them, their families may be falling apart from emotional neglect.

Workaholics don't look across the net—they stare! That stare accuses their partners of getting in their way, slowing them down, making unreasonable demands. They wonder why their mates can't understand that their work just takes this much time. Why can't they understand this and let them be?

On their own side of the net, however, loneliness is eating away at them. If workaholics looked at themselves first, might they not realize that their partners' demands are not unreasonable? Might they not come to see that the hole they are trying to fill cannot be satisfied with more work, more money, more things? Can't they see that there is no such thing as peace by acquisition?

Workaholics are not simply people who work a lot. They are incapable of not working. Their goal is not to achieve something, but simply to work. The payoffs may be enormous; but once the pattern of workaholism starts to affect the quality of our relationships, we have some choices to make.

TASK: Where do Workaholic patterns fit in your life? Reflect on the six skills of a Stage II relationship (pages 49 to 54) and then score yourself from 1 (not at all) to 10 (very much) according to how much you act out the role of the Workaholic in any given relationship. Then write a paragraph in which you outline the consequences of this sort of behavior in a relationship.

The Perfectionist

The Perfectionist's self-image is based on doing things "well enough." Unfortunately, to the Perfectionist "well enough" means "perfectly." But since nothing on earth is perfect, Perfectionists are locked in a terrible cycle of always having to do better. No matter how much or how well they have performed, it is never enough.

And they not only view themselves this way—Perfectionists look at everyone else that way too. Nothing anyone else does is ever done well enough. What is being played out here, as in all of these patterns, is the same set of expectations foisted on them (and hated by them) when they were children.

Perfectionists look across the net and wonder why their mates care so little about quality and success. Riveted to their own set of perceptions, which they think of as normal, Perfectionists resent their partners for being sloppy and unwilling to cooperate. Living with a Perfectionist is therefore frustrating and degrading, since it means trying to live up to impossible standards.

Unless Perfectionists are willing to first consider what's going on on their side of the net, their relationships won't improve. They need to learn that it is reasonable to be satisfied with the best they or anyone else can do; that's all that can be asked. It is reasonable to request—no, demand—that Perfectionists learn to relax and free themselves from the impossible, self-imposed demands of their passion for perfection.

TASK: Are you a Perfectionist? To what degree? Reflect on the six skills of a Stage II relationship (pages 49 to 54), and then score yourself from 1 (not at all) to 10 (very much) according to how much you act out the role of the Perfectionist in any given relationship. Then write a paragraph in which you outline the consequences of this sort of behavior in a relationship.

The Tap Dancer

Tap Dancers are terrified of commitment, so they run from any working relationship as soon as commitment comes up. If Tap Dancers are also People-Pleasers, they will most often be less than honest about why they are ending the relationship. Rather than admit that they're not ready for, willing, or able to deal with commitment, they fabricate other reasons: You're too short, too tall, too smart, not smart enough; you ask too much, take too much, demand too much, fight too much. Maybe it's your red hair.

If a Tap Dancer's partner is tied into one of these patterns, he or she is liable to take these reasons at face value and try to change the offending characteristic; but it's all to no avail. The issue is the nonrecovering Tap Dancer, who is dancing away from commitment, while the blind partner is running down the wrong road.

When Tap Dancers look across the net, it's often with pain in their hearts and tears in their eyes. Often enough they want intimacy, love, and connectedness; but the experience of commitment is so painful to them that they can't follow through. They bitterly complain about the emptiness in their lives, but at the same time they enter relationships that can tolerate no intimacy or walk away from those that could.

TASK: Does the Tap Dancer pattern fit you? Reflect on the six skills of a Stage II relationship (pages 49 to 54), and then score yourself from 1 (not at all) to 10 (very much) according to how much you act out the role of the Tap Dancer in any given relationship. Then write a paragraph in which you outline the consequences of this sort of behavior in a relationship.

If, as you worked your way through these pages, you found yourself creeping toward despair with the feeling, "Oh my God, I'm all of it," relax. Each of us probably has a little bit of all these patterns in our lives. It's just a matter of degree.

The point is not that we're "sick." We do not therefore "deserve" any unhappiness we have in our relationships. (Nor does it mean that we're "healthy" and therefore qualify for unending happiness if we don't.) The question is not if or if not, it's how much and where.

If we don't recognize the patterns, they will continue to create consequences in our lives. But once we discern the pattern, we can start to make effective decisions. The first decision has to be about us; it has to concern our side of the net. Later decisions may concern the relationship, but for now the issue is me. Do I play fair?

What do I need to look at and possibly change if I am to be a more trustworthy partner?

There's no guarantee, of course, that if you are willing to be honest with yourself and start this process, your partner will follow suit. Such is the risk of relationships. But starting with yourself and becoming the healthiest person you can be is the most effective, most powerful strategy there is to "get someone else to change." Risky as it may be, you can show your partner, by giving him or her a glimpse at the serenity and quality of your life, that there's a better way. Games between people are played only as long as they continue to work. When they're no longer acceptable to one of the partners, that game comes to an end. At least one possible option then is to say, "Let's find something better."

Chapter 4

UNDERSTANDING YOUR PARTNER:
THE OTHER SIDE OF THE NET

Just as there can't be a tennis match without two players, there is no such thing as a one-person relationship. A relationship requires the space between, and "between" requires two realities.

The easy part of a relationship is loving and caring about another person. The difficult part is filling that space between with enough light, so that when the darkness threatens it never fully conquers. This requires the energy and concern of both partners. Once you've made the commitment to take care of your side of the net on an ongoing basis, the next step is to reach out to your partner.

Relationships, as we know, are built on trust and thrive on gift-giving, and no gift builds more trust than reaching out your mind and heart in a genuine effort to understand. Just as communicating does not require agreeing, understanding another does not mean giving permission for things to continue as they are. Understanding creates patience; and the more understanding we possess (and we possess it by caring enough to try to understand), the more compassion we are able to extend.

When Nancy understood her partner enough to realize that he might very well misinterpret her efforts at personal growth as a rejection of him, she was able to alleviate his fears. When my friend, the mother of a fearful daughter, understood her small daughter's fears and her need to be assured that she had a home, she created the love club.

Do you understand what your partner fears deep in the night, and what gifts, no matter how small, light up your partner's soul? Do you know what experiences form your partner's perceptions of the important and not so important elements of your relationship? It is all too easy, when your partner is communicating or trying to communicate with you, to say, "It is not important," "You are not important," "That isn't the way I see things, so you must be wrong." Every negative response increases the distance and the distrust in a relationship.

But we have choices. If we choose to, we can respond to our partner's revelations with words, body language, and gestures that say, "I hear you. I may not agree or see it that way, but I grant you the right to be different." We can say, "Yes, you are different and thank God you are, for it gives me a chance to learn something from another's perceptions."

We can respond in any number of ways that increase intimacy by generating hospitality and thus trust. When we respond in these ways, we invite others to tell us more. A great deal of it comes down to listening.

Listening

Someone once told me some interesting facts about listening. When we're listening, most of us:

- hear only about half of what is said
- understand only about half of what we hear
- remember only about half of what we understand
- make appropriate judgments on only about half of what we remember, and
- act appropriately on only about half of that.

When we take all of those halves into consideration, there isn't much left that generates hospitality. At critical moments in conversation with others, we either shut them off or remain open and truly invite them into our lives. To a large extent, the quality of our relationships depends on what we do in those critical moments. Four major obstacles can block the path of listening:

1. *Fear.* Fear of closeness, fear of rejection, fear of success, fear of just about anything. We resist what we fear.
2. *Busyness.* Listening takes time and requires that we do nothing else but listen. Being too busy necessarily makes listening impossible.
3. *Resentments.* Since resentment is a closed door, you can't harbor resentment and practice the art of being open at the same time.
4. *Bad habits.* To a greater or lesser degree, any of the behavioral patterns listed in the previous chapter will effectively block genuine listening.

Good listeners have looked at these obstacles and overcome them. But that is part of taking care of *their* side of the net. The issue here is turning an open head and heart to the other.

We Are Not the Same

As obvious as this statement may be, we don't always act as if we believe or understand it. More often than not, our attitudes and behavior say, "If you are different, you are wrong."

One of the differences between us, of course, is that some of us are male and others female. This is both a physiological and an experiential difference. In our culture, little boys and little girls are raised as if they're in different worlds; they are taught different lessons, treated differently, and have vastly different expectations laid upon them. Boys and girls do not come to define the world and their place in it in the same ways, and therefore the options that both see as realistic or even desirable are different. This does not mean, of course, that these differences make one sex superior to the other; nor are the differences necessarily desirable. But they're often real, and it's critically important to building a healthy relationship that we try to understand what those different life experiences were for our partners and how those experiences helped form the way they see and act in the world.

The chart below has proven to be a powerful door-opener in the quest for improved communications. Allowing for great differences in background, the following are valid generalizations.

Women are raised to do the following:

1. Please others—it will make you feel good.
2. Act in response to others' needs.
3. Wait—others must initiate.
4. Look good—but you can never look good enough.
5. Remember that people count, and their feelings and goals count more than yours.
6. Know that not too much is expected of you—results are not essential.
7. Serve; be of use to others.
8. Place a high value on romance—Prince Charming is on the way.
9. Don't risk; it's how others fail.
10. Receiving is acceptable; people will give you things.

Men are raised to do the following:

1. Win—it will make you feel good.
2. Be independent; do it yourself.
3. Be tough: don't cry, don't let others know how you feel.
4. Never surrender—when you give in, you have failed.
5. Production counts—you didn't try hard enough if you didn't get the results.
6. Life is tough; you must be able to endure tough times.
7. You are successful if you have things to show.
8. Control things around you; your wants count.
9. Risk—it is the door to success.
10. Never receive; receiving makes you dependent.

Following the line of reasoning that grows out of such experiences, here are some common criteria of strength and goodness.

Young women growing up learn that they are good or strong when they:

- serve
- care
- are people-centered
- are religious
- help their partners

They are bad or weak when they are:

- assertive
- tough-minded
- goal-oriented
- competitive
- opinionated

Young men growing up learn that they are good or strong when they:

- do it alone
- are emotional rocks
- never give in
- win by manipulation or power
- succeed

They are bad or weak when they:

- need help
- break down and ask for help
- receive
- surrender
- share

Admittedly, these criteria don't fit all men and all women. They are but general guidelines intended to help us look across the net at our partners.

Task: Down Memory Lane

I suggest that you and your partner stroll down memory lane and take a long, hard look. Each of you should pick out the criterion above that most seems to apply to you. Then follow these steps:

1. Write out an incident or event in your life in which you acted out this attitude or belief.
2. Reflecting on that event, describe how you felt about it.
3. Reflecting on these first two questions, consider if there's a relation between what you practiced back then and how you tend to think, act, and feel today.
4. Consider if you have seen a pattern stretching from yesterday to today. Assuming that you want to change that pattern, how do you feel when you try?
5. Share what you've written with each other so that you can learn something about how you and your partner each experience the world differently.

Here's an example of this exercise from the work my wife and I have done. My wife is frequently frustrated and mystified by (if not downright angry at) my too-small ability to share feelings, admit weakness, receive help, admit her into my life as a helpmate. We both know that I don't especially want to be this way. I surely don't want to hurt her or diminish the quality of the life we share. So what is the problem? Why has it been hard for me to comply with her all-too-reasonable requests and expectations? I didn't know and neither did she. I knew it wasn't the result of simple meanness, but I wasn't sure my wife knew that. A bridge of understanding was necessary. Like all communication, it would take straight talk and honest listening. So I followed the exercise described above, and here is what I came up with.

1. *Event.* One of the rules in our house for boys (girls had different rules) was, "Be tough!" We were taught that when boys got to be five years old, they were men and no more crying

was allowed. If you broke the rule by crying, you got a crack on the head; but even worse was the knowledge that you let the powers-that-be down. The real penalty was shame.

2. *Feelings.* The only feeling I could identify was enormous pride at not crying. No matter what happened at school or on the playground, I couldn't be hurt badly enough to cry, and I felt very good about that. I loved it!

3. *Then and today.* Of course, I saw a relation. The very skills and abilities my wife demanded and expected of me were the exact opposite of what I'd been practicing most of my life. She wanted me to confess when I was hurt or in need. My inner "muscles," developed over forty years of constant practice, said, "Never." So deeply ingrained were those patterns and so powerful those psychic muscles that often, bleeding or not, stressed to collapse or not, I didn't know I was hurt or in need.

4. *Feelings about change.* My head says, "Of course you want to change, since it's the sane thing to do," but sharing still feels uncomfortable to me. When I challenge the old rules, I feel the same shame, the same guilt, the same sense of failure I felt forty years ago. The difference is that I now recognize what is going on, and those old feelings have lost a lot of power.

5. *Sharing with my partner.* My wife knew none of this until I told her. In fact, I knew little enough about the patterns and processes until I sat down, took hold of pen and paper, and actually did the work.

My wife and I worked through not just this one event, but many. The more I worked out and shared, the more she understood this flawed, trapped, in-the-present-but-facing-the-past person she married. What she learned about me didn't make my inabilities any more acceptable, but it did make them more understandable—to both of us. And with that understanding came the hospitality and patience that are necessary in building trust.

Significant Words

Since we both enjoyed the rewards of sharing these sorts of experiences, my wife and I developed a technique designed to help us be more specific. It revolves around significant words.

It took us several years to realize that a big part of the difficulty we had in communicating was our assumption that the words we commonly used had the same meaning for each of us. In fact, they didn't mean the same thing at all, and our assumption that they did led to all sorts of problems.

The need to develop this technique grew out of the reality surrounding the word *shopping*. How could there possibly be more than one meaning of this word? To me, shopping means you go somewhere to buy something. The sooner you get it done, the better; so as soon as you get what you want, you face the door and go through it as quickly as possible. That is shopping. How could it possibly mean anything else?

It would be understating the fact to say that a certain amount of confusion grew up around our different perceptions of the word. But when my wife described what this word specifically meant to her, I finally understood—to my utter amazement—that she *enjoys* shopping. She looks forward to it. I also learned that "buying" does not necessarily have anything to do with shopping. Apparently, the fascination is just with looking; my wife has no qualms about trying clothes on that she has no intention of buying at the time, even though such behavior seemed terribly rude and a total waste of time to me.

As my wife shared with me the events of her past, I came to understand that she, her sisters, and her mother often planned shopping parties, just to give them a chance to get together. They love it; it's neither a burden nor a contest to see how quickly the task can get done. If it takes all day, who cares? But until I was willing to understand this, I had no idea what shopping meant to my wife; and once I understood, meaningful compromises could be made that not only safeguarded trust but increased it.

This exercise takes two people, since you can't very well understand more about your partner if your partner isn't willing to share what she or he knows or feels. Sometimes it's difficult to share, because what you have to say has its roots in a painful experience. Often, however, it is not. People generally love to talk about themselves if they're given half a chance. The trick is to return the gift of listening after you've spoken.

Here's a list of words that my wife and I have discussed as we have attempted to find out what's on each other's side of the net. It's far from complete, of course, but you can add to it or subtract from it to suit your needs.

- intimacy
- vacation
- security
- sharing feelings
- abuse
- competition
- friendship
- prayer
- touch
- risk
- wife
- children

- romance
- money
- sex
- vulnerability
- rights
- space
- meals
- love
- marriage
- men
- husband
- play

- being on time
- saving
- feelings
- time off
- failure
- trust
- God
- respect
- commitment
- women
- discipline
- work

The list is endless. Whenever an issue surfaces in your relationship, there's a word to name it—and you and your partner probably interpret that word differently. When we lack any understanding of our partners' experiences and feelings, we tend to judge them by our own lights and hurt them by assuming that they experience the world the same way we do.

As we will see in more detail in the next chapter, an essential ingredient of successful sharing is to begin with the right attitude. The right attitude here is the honest attempt to understand the other—not in order to judge, criticize, or manipulate, but to reach out, open up, and hear who your partner is.

Beyond Understanding

After understanding, then what? So he wants more sex and you want more sharing of feelings? We both understand where the other is coming from, but we still want what we want. Now what?

Compromise. The call for genuine love, spiritual maturity, and the pivotal point of a healthy relationship: the realization that if we feed one another, neither of us ever has to be hungry again.

Chapter 5

MAKING CONTACT

Now you have learned to set the rules, been encouraged to evaluate your own side of the net, and seen some techniques that will enable you to gain further understanding of your partner. The next task is to make contact—to communicate. We will look at two uses of communication: as a means to understand one another; and for conflict resolution, since there will be conflict even in a relationship where communication is of the highest order. Learning to handle conflict in a positive manner is in itself an important form of communication.

The Three As

The foundations necessary for successful communication are the three As: attitude, atmosphere, and ability.

Attitude

If you attempt to communicate when your attitude or your partner's attitude is bad, the whole enterprise is doomed to failure. It is far better simply to refrain from contact rather than risk the rejection and the bad feelings about a relationship that often result from such attempts to communicate.

Let's look at some attitudes that can poison communication.

Superiority

This attitude proclaims, "I will communicate with you for as long as it takes me to persuade you that I am right." "Right," of course, means seeing things from the "superior" person's point of view. (A variation of this is the "Genius-to-Idiot" game that will be discussed in the next chapter.) What usually motivates this attitude is either enormous pride, or fear that attempts to masquerade as competence. Either way, there is no room for another's point of view, so communication dies.

Competition

This attitude demands not truth or fairness but a winner, and it is also often motivated by fear. Some people perceive themselves as always having to give in, always getting the short end of the stick, always being ripped off; they are not only angry but terrified that "it will happen again." They may have endured the trauma of a failed relationship in which they have been hurt so badly and used so shamefully they are going to make darn sure no one has the chance to get the upper hand on them ever again. Thus every request for compliance or cooperation, no matter how reasonable, is held up to the questionable light of these past experiences. In communication, if one has to win and the other has to lose, both lose.

Anger

You cannot truly communicate with another if you are full of anger. You can communicate *that* you are angry, you can communicate with brute clarity that your partner is not safe around you; but this is not the kind of contact this chapter advocates.

I see this attitude in a forty-seven-year-old woman I know who grew up in an alcoholic family. She suffered no physical or sexual abuse during her childhood, but she did experience great emotional abuse. Only she didn't know it was abuse then; it was just "normal." Now she knows, and her anger blots out any other consideration.

This woman has been married for twenty-seven of her forty-seven years, and until recently her husband thought they were doing just fine. But as his wife became aware of her past heritage and the examples of continuing abuse she perceived in her marriage, he increasingly became the target of her rage, none of which he understood. Since both were coming to counseling, I assumed that both were willing to try some new techniques; but it didn't take long to demonstrate the invalidity of that assumption. This woman bluntly stated it was her "season to be angry." She didn't want to compromise, discuss, communicate, or try to see anyone else's point. At least she was honest.

There was no point in striving to communicate in such a situation. Her husband could only do all that he could to take care of his side of the net and wait to see what his partner was going to do. For her part, she had to accept the possibility that a consequence of her staying cocooned in her anger might be that her husband would decide he couldn't wait any longer. They were in a foot race to see if his patience and love would win out over her anger.

Minimal Importance

This attitude shouts, "I will humor you if I must, but I don't take this all that seriously." Sometimes this attitude is pervasive; one of the partners may never take either the communication or the issues very seriously. Other times it's episodic; one partner has no time to discuss a specific issue that's of major importance to the other. Either way, no behavior more successfully discounts another person than taking lightly what is of significant importance to him or her. Nothing destroys trust more effectively. If an issue is important to one person in a relationship, it's important to the relationship.

If these are destructive attitudes, what might creative attitudes be? I would like to suggest three attitudes that have long been taught as healthy.

Willingness

Being willing is the bedrock of communication; you can't communicate with someone who won't communicate with you. And since communication, as we shall soon see, often leads to action, being willing also indicates the desire to do what needs to be done to validate the communication process—to follow up when it's time to show that it *does* do some good to talk and that soaring expectations *can* come true.

Honesty

This means an attitude that refuses to hide behind rationalization, blaming, or alibis. Honesty means I talk straight with my feelings and perceptions. Honesty means that when I catch myself playing a game, I admit it and ask forgiveness. Only in honesty can you face another and see who is there. Only in honesty can you expect to have a fair hearing and get a fair response.

Openness

This means being willing to learn. Openness means I acknowledge that there is more than one way—my way. Openness means that without losing my integrity I am willing to listen to your side of this issue and possibly learn something. Like parachutes, minds and communication only work when they are open.

Atmosphere

If the participants are old pros with a great deal of skill, then where and when they communicate is less important. But for novices or those who are trying to communicate their way through a history of failure and hurt, setting is most important.

Check out the time and place. Do not attempt to communicate if one or both are so tired you can hardly think. Communication is too important to attempt when you're not at your best. Also, don't begin a session if you are too busy or trying to do several things at the same time. Trying to communicate while you're reading the paper, talking on the phone, or feeding the kids may clearly say to your partner, "This is not important to me."

Where are you going to communicate? My wife and I have found that our home is usually not the place for these formal communication sessions. It's too busy. Kids are coming and going, phones are ringing, and people are stopping over for any number of reasons. Instead, a neighborhood restaurant within walking distance of our home is our communication place.

Timing is everything in communication, as in most things. Pick the right time, pick the right place, come with the right attitude, and only good things can happen. Our schedules are busy, but we have designated every Friday morning as our communication time. That is when we share and pick what word we are going to discuss in the coming week.

Enter willing. Many couples acknowledge the importance of communication but immediately find a dozen reasons why it wouldn't work for them. They are too busy, there is no good time, everyone is always too tired. Whatever the reasons for not communicating, if it is not done, there will be consequences. If the relationship is of sufficient importance, a right time can and must be found.

Where is a good place for you? What is the right time?

Ability

It is no coincidence that the skills necessary for successful communication are the same as those that are essential for a healthy relationship. Successful communication demands that both people are able to talk straight about feelings and needs, and that both are free enough of obstacles to honestly listen.

In previous chapters, I have outlined some effective communication techniques, which I'll briefly review below along with a new technique. In a later chapter, I will outline a very specific program for generating and deepening communication. These programs are bonding exercises. Any and all of them, when used in the spirit of the three As, will increase communication by increasing trust. Ultimately, communication is trust in action.

1. *Sentence completion* (outlined in chapter 2). Each person completes these sentences for his or her partner. Be specific and make sure your responses are about behaviors.

- When you _____, I feel most loved, cared about, valued.
- When you _____, I feel most unloved, devalued, discounted.

As mentioned before, once this data has been honestly exchanged, the way to improve trust and communication is clear.

2. *Using significant words as communication starters* (outlined in chapter 4). Once the attitude, atmosphere, and ability are established, you can put this exercise to excellent use. Pick your word a week ahead of time. Think and write about that chosen word from your viewpoint, and come prepared to the appointed place at the appointed time.

3. *Gift-giving.* This has two parts. First, pick the right time and thank each other for a gift given that day. The gift need not be tangible. It may be a smile, a kind word, a compliment, a chore done without nagging. Doing this forces you to hone two skills: the ability to be grateful (which helps fight against the tendency to take your partner's gifts for granted), and an awareness of the importance of giving gifts. If you arrive at the appointed time and your partner says, "I'd like to thank you for a gift today, but there were none that I could see," you had better shape up. No matter how secure you may feel in the relationship, if you don't bring a present to the party, often enough the party will end.

The second half of this technique is to then ask your partner for a gift for the coming day. Again, this doesn't have to be an object. You might say, "There is a big meeting tomorrow, and I would appreciate it if you would ask me how it went when I get home." It may be the other side of that coin: "I'd appreciate it if you would tell me how it went without my having to go at you with a crowbar to pry it out of you." This part of the technique helps you become aware that your partner has needs, and it forces you to develop the ability to ask for what you need.

One last comment about communication. When we communicate, it is not simply what *we say* that matters; it is what *they heard*. What your partner heard may very well not be what you said or meant. Your partner isn't necessarily twisting your words; maybe he or she just doesn't have the background or experience to receive what you are sending. If you are not sure that what was heard was what you said, check it out with the following five steps.

1. *Clearly know what you want to say.* If what you want to say is important, practice putting words to your thoughts before you try to communicate with your partner. Do the words truly convey your meaning? Are you saying what you mean? Can you say it in several different ways? In counseling sessions I have often encountered verbal explosions; but even though a lot of emotion was involved, it was not at all clear what the individual was trying to communicate. Note: It is hard to take seriously and respect someone who cannot verbalize what he or she is trying to communicate.

2. *Make physical contact.* Make sure you are looking at the person you're communicating with, and that your partner is looking at you. Make sure the newspapers are down, the TV's turned off, and the chairs are positioned so you can see one another. Physical contact can also help. Touch knees, hold hands. It is another, powerful bridge that will promote communication and good will while the words are being said.

3. *Talk straight.* Don't beat around the bush, use double-talk, or couch your words in so many qualifiers that the meaning is blurred. If you need something, ask for it. If you feel or felt a certain way, put the best word to it you know. If your feelings were hurt, say so. Don't say, "Well, kind of, but I'm not sure, possibly there was a little bit of something . . ."

Remember, if you don't talk straight, chances are small you will ever be heard.

4. *Get feedback.* Once you have spoken as clearly as you can, ask your partner to repeat what you said. Each statement we make has two parts: feeling and content. In each statement, we tell the other person what is involved and how we feel about it. Proper feedback includes both. It is one thing to receive feedback that says, "Yes I heard you. I didn't show up for your sister's birthday party." It is another to say that same thing and also add, "and I hear that you are terribly angry, feel betrayed, and want to wring my neck." Did your partner hear both the affect and the content? Of course he or she may hear very well, feed it back to you, and then say, "But I don't care." That is a whole different issue. Then you have to make a decision; but at least it will be based on clearly communicated information.

5. *Thank your partner.* Communication is a gift. Giving someone strict attention, truly trying to hear not only what that person has to say but who he or she is, is a most precious gift. Even a partner who couldn't exactly understand what you said at least tried and deserves a thank you. Everyone loves to be appreciated. Our gifts need to be acknowledged. When they are, it increases the chances that they will be given again.

Conflict Resolution

One form of communication is dialogue. Its goal is not to find and solve problems, but to share yourself honestly with another person. Through dialogue, however, conflicts will often come to light. It is one thing to understand, but another thing to answer the question, "What do we do about it?"

"You want more sex and I want more sharing of feelings. We both understand each other's needs, backgrounds, and meanings. Great. But what do we do?" Here are some steps.

These steps are techniques, but the technique is less important than the attitude. There are no quick fixes, instant cures, or easy answers. Resolving conflict is a skill that demands practice, attention, and lots of good will—on both parts. Here is a way to arrive at a resolution that leaves the relationship stronger, not weaker.

1. *Clearly identify the issue.* What is the conflict about? As easy as this sounds, it is not. Often the real issue may be a bruised ego or the feeling that you're being railroaded into accepting a condition you don't agree with. Often, on close scrutiny, the real issue is seen to be some character defect that has deep roots in a family-of-origin experience and is still being acted out.

   Any of these real issues may be at the core of the *apparent* issue—dealing with your children, spending your money, being on time, sharing housework, and so forth.

   So, first clarify the issue. Know what the conflict is truly about.

2. *State each other's point.* Once the issue has been identified, it is important that each of you verbalize your partner's point. Listen to what is being told to you, and try to repeat it without judgment. Again, your attitude is critical here. If you responded, "I hear what you are saying, but you're wrong. You should not feel that way," the process will end.

3. *Acknowledge the validity of your partner's point.* In some situations, once the issue has been clarified and each person has had a chance to verbalize the other's point, it becomes clear that there can be no resolution, because it would violate someone's values and integrity to bend or compromise on the issue. Such an issue may be a "relationship-buster" and has to be dealt with accordingly.

   Many times, however, each of you will be able to say, "Yes, I can see why you feel what you do. I can understand that my point of view is not the only valid one. I can hear what you're saying." From there, progress can be made.

4. *Determine what your partner is asking of you.* Here is where you benefit from working through the first three steps. Now there is light to work with, not just heat. Once the issues are clarified and validated, most people find that what their partners are asking of them is quite reasonable.

5. *State your own point.* In your effort to extend yourself to understand your partner, it is important not to lose sight of your own point. If that happens, one partner may compromise his or her integrity and feel the resentment later on. All too often, adult children of dysfunctional families, who often grew up in shame-based environments, start to feel very guilty when they ask for what they need. It is especially important for such people to clearly understand their point and reaffirm to themselves that they have a right to it.

6. *Acknowledge whether your point is valid.* At this stage of the process, you may come to understand that your point is rooted in some old, neurotic patterns and may not be valid at all. You may be demanding, for instance, that your children obey you instantly and always, or you may be asking your partner to make you feel loved and important—always.

   On the other hand, on reflection, you may come to the conclusion that your point is valid; it is still true and reasonable to you.

7. *Determine what you are asking of your partner.* If you don't know specifically what you're asking of the other person, you can hardly expect him or her to respond in a suitable manner. Light, not just heat; lucid, specific requests, not just nebulous wounded feelings.

8. *Outline some possible solutions.* Solutions and resolutions here are always a matter of compromise, but compromise should be looked upon as a "win-win" situation, not with an attitude that says, "Let's see how much I can keep from losing." If the previous work has been done properly, it's often relatively easy to comply with what your partner wants, as long as you can also get what you want and need.

No one is perfect, and there are no instant cures. Understand that whatever you ask of your partner, however small, may be difficult for your partner to give. Be patient in the presence of good intentions. If your partner is not living up to an agreement, but is still trying, give him or her the benefit of the doubt. Don't make it a crime to fail.

As we make contact across the net, trust is generated and deepened. And trust is the name of the game.

Chapter 6

DEALING WITH FAILING AND FAILED RELATIONSHIPS

By this time there should be no particular mystery why relationships fail. They fail because the people in them don't have the skills or the willingness to learn the skills necessary for success.

Healthy relationships are made of trust, and when trust ends, the games start. Relationships are living things and can therefore die. When games persist too long, the end of the relationship will soon follow. The people in it may not physically move apart, but the relationship dies all the same.

Although the games that emerge in failed and failing relationships are too subtle and numerous ever to be catalogued completely, here are some of the more common forms.

The "Genius-to-Idiot" Game

This game assumes that in all communication or interaction between two people there must be a genius and an idiot—there is no room for common ground or mutual learning. And the dynamic always plays out in the same way: If I must be the genius, you must be the idiot; if I must be right, you must be wrong; if I must be the winner, you must be the loser. Has anyone ever tried to relate to you with these ground rules? It may be your partner in a relationship, or anyone else—a car mechanic, a waitress, a lawyer, whatever. The effect is always the same. When the genius-to-idiot game is played, you've got several responses.

- You can get angry and explode in a cynical, aggressive, or disparaging way.
- You can get angry but turn it inside and become depressed, withdrawn, self-pitying, and just plain apathetic.
- You can accept the role of idiot and become passive and brainless and refuse to think or make any decisions.

Any such response may trigger an unhealthy response:

- Your partner may become angry in response to your anger, or indignant that you would get angry at someone who is merely pointing out your faults.
- Your partner may become critical of your silence and irritated by your depression. While you are feeling powerless, your partner accuses you of deliberately having no energy and wonders, often out loud, why you are sabotaging the relationship.
- Your partner may complain that he or she is the only one who thinks around here. He or she may feel abused by being forced to make all the decisions because you are unwilling or unable to take the responsibility to make them yourself.

In the end, game responds to game, layer upon layer, until all trust is smothered and straight talk is twisted. If you ever speak of the situation candidly to mutual friends or perhaps a minister or counselor, what comes across loud and clear is that your partner "needs to change." If you're fortunate, your therapeutic process will get you to start looking at your side of the net. What changes could you possibly make that would break this pattern?

The "You Decide" Game

This game is played out when one partner asks the other any question that requires a decision. Should we go to a show tonight? Which one? Should we paint the house this year or next year or never? Should we try to communicate with these techniques or not? The answer is invariably the same: "I don't know. What do you think? You decide." The response to this game can be any of the following:

- You can stop asking and take the sole responsibility for any decision.
- You can refuse to make any decisions and simply watch nothing ever get done.
- You can get revenge by making sure the decisions you make are as repugnant to the irresponsible partner as possible. If he or she hates bright red paint, everything in sight becomes red. If your partner has been waiting a long time for a specific TV program, wait till that night to invite company over.

And the partner will respond in kind:

- He or she may retreat even further, if that is possible, into the mental and physical "do not disturb" zone.
- He or she may fly into a rage about the decisions you make.
- He or she may constantly insult you for not making any decisions.

Fair? Of course not. And when people do not play fair, trust slips away.

The Guessing Game

The Guessing game is what happens when one partner will not provide important information. How do you feel? What do you want to do? What do you want for your birthday? Did you like last Thursday's gathering? All questions—no answers. Guessing is all that is left.

It doesn't take a genius to figure out if you guess wrong and act in a way that your partner does not appreciate, you will be blamed. How can you trust someone who operates in this way? The answer is, you can't. There goes trust.

The responses to this game are varied but not necessarily different than the responses to any other game. If you relate to this game, work out the details as they appear in your personal situation:

When this game of Guessing is played on you, what you do?

1.

2.

3.

And then how does your partner respond?

1.

2.

3.

Before your eyes will appear the blueprint of a failing relationship. Each reaction not provided with honesty and in trust helps bury your chances for happiness.

The "We-Can't-Afford-It" Game

Games are games because they are dishonest, so there's no game being played if you truly cannot afford to buy something. The game becomes destructive, however, when no matter what is asked for, planned, or thought about, the answer is always the same: "We can't afford it."

The game can be played out even after you've bought something or gone somewhere. While you're on vacation, you may constantly hear things like, "Don't get orange juice, we can't afford it" or

"Don't think about taking that tour, we can't afford it." You get the idea.

If this game sounds familiar to you, fill in the blanks with how you respond:

1.

2.

3.

One response, of course, is to punish the other person by buying so many things that you truly do go broke. You might stockpile a hundred bars of soap and use the excuse that you got them on sale so you really were saving money, when what you actually were doing was running up a major league bill just to get even.

And then how does your partner respond?

1.

2.

3.

Year after year, game after game, layer upon layer, the relationship dies.

The Seduction-Rejection Game

This game can be played out on many fronts. The essential feature is that one person seductively lures the other into trusting him or her. The seduction may be physical or it may be verbal; compliments, affirmations, and other gestures of acceptance are powerful seducers, especially if the other person suffers from a sense of inadequacy to start with. Lonely people are terribly vulnerable.

Once the hope has flamed and trust is established, then the fire is doused. The rejection may not be deliberate; it may come because your partner suffers from a terrible fear of intimacy. Although the seduction felt good, he or she soon starts reacting in all the old, destructive ways. Rather than compliments, there are complaints; rather than invitations, there is neglect; rather than sharing, there are closed doors. You're baffled by the constant turn-it-on, turn-it-off charm, sweetness and acceptance.

If you find yourself constantly falling victim to this kind of "peacock," the first order of business is not to condemn your partner, but to find out why you are so vulnerable to this game.

How do you respond to the seduction-rejection game?

1.

2.

3.

And how does your partner respond when you have acted out that response?

1.

2.

3.

Then what happens? Depending on the degree of insight and your willingness to work on your own program, either the same pattern keeps being played out your entire life, or you break it.

The "My-Rights-Are-Mine, Yours-We'll-Talk-About" Game

As the name implies, this game is about one-sided benefits. The one who is on the short end of this game feels like a small child who has to get permission to exercise his or her natural rights. It is terribly degrading at anytime to have to beg, but especially when what you're begging for is yours by rights and you're having to beg from someone you gave your trust to.

In its financial form, this game has a slightly different name, "My Money Is Mine, Yours We'll Talk About." If you didn't set up clear and specific ground rules about money when you entered the relationship (and this is especially important if it's a second marriage for either of you), money is bound to be a problem. Sadly, this is often the case.

As this game is played out, how might you react?

1.

2.

3.

How does your partner react in response?

1.,

2.

3.

As game feeds on game and distrust generates more distrust, the relationship dies. It can only be saved if both people are willing to stop playing games and start playing fair.

Using Sex as a Reward or Punishment

Sex is a language, a way to say something. Like liturgy in a church service, it is for the purpose of expressing what is already there. It is a deep, sacred way of saying, "I care, I trust, I love." When couples have sexual problems, in my experience, it almost always suggests that they no longer have anything to say to one another; sex is the only thing going for them. And though assuredly sex can be thrilling and exciting, when it's an end unto itself and ceases to be a sacrament of shared meaning, loneliness and emptiness are often the result.

When sex is used as a reward or punishment—when it's offered or withheld depending on what someone has done or failed to do—it is stripped of its symbolic ability to say anything of value, and trust is always the victim. Sex without romance and sensitivity is like liturgy without faith.

When you perceive sex is being used as a weapon or a reward, how might you react?

1.

2.

3.

And when you behave in this manner, how does your partner respond?

1.

2.

3.

What can be done about the game-responding-to-game pattern? There is only one answer. Begin with yourself. Stop playing this game, or any game, and begin to build trust stone by stone until a solid highway is established. The only way you know exactly which stones are required by your mate is by asking—not assuming.

The "Ain't It Awful" Game

This game is a favorite of negative people. For awfulizers, things are never bad, they're terrible! It is never just hot, it is boiling! They are never low on cash, they are totally bankrupt! When they're disappointed, they say they're devastated. When something nice happens, they hardly notice it.

Adult children of dysfunctional families, of course, are terribly vulnerable to this game. They have learned by word and example that life *is* awful. So many terrible things have happened to them that it's hard to consider or expect that anything not awful would happen in their lives.

Awfulizers also tend to exaggerate in the extreme (when they so choose) anything that might be said to them. If you say, "I feel lonely," they blow it out of all proportion and respond, "Why are you telling me I am a bad person who is never present to you?" If you announce, "We have some issues to work on," they complain, "Why are you telling me I am a terrible husband or wife? Why are you so dissatisfied with this relationship that you want to end it?"

That may be the very last thing you said or meant. But if that is what they hear, filtered through their old, neurotic tapes, then that is what they will respond with. And you are stuck.

Awfulizers find it almost impossible to conceive that any truly lovely thing could happen to them. And while winning is foreign to an awfulizer, the most important thing that could happen to such a person in this life would be to get involved in a healthy, nurturing relationship. But if things get too good in a relationship, an awfulizer will create a crisis of some kind or other to bring things back to "normal." Thus the couple goes from one crisis to another, none of which are necessary, none of which are out of their control—like a tornado or an auto accident—and none of which are caused by anything but the awfulizer's need for pain.

Awfulizers are like that. Often one of the partners gets tired of all the chaos and confusion and says adios. How do you trust someone who needs chaos to feel normal!

How might a person react to an awfulizer?

1.

2.

3.

How does the awfulizer respond?

1.

2.

3.

You can't do anything about an awfulizer any more than you can do anything about anyone who is stuck in a game. The consequences, however, are guaranteed—the death of trust.

Expectations

Perhaps the most important lesson to be learned by studying these games and their corresponding responses is the importance of realistic expectations. If one person in a relationship is so rooted in a destructive pattern that it's impossible to practice the skills necessary for a healthy relationship, and if that person's partner has expectations of a rational, open, loving life, hearts will invariably be broken. People can't give what they don't have.

Nonrecovering alcoholics or other addictive people are often incapable of functioning in healthy relationships. That is not to say that they are incapable of loving. They may very well love; in fact, the pain and shame of loving those they reject and play games on often causes them to continue the addictive behavior, since addictions medicate pain. Thus the lie of all addictions perpetuates itself. I love but I hurt the very ones I love. To blot out that pain I use my addiction to cope. But the acting out of that addiction only deepens the addiction and worsens my self-centeredness. Thus I feel a greater need to protect myself from the love I sense I do not deserve, so I reject those who love me, which creates a greater need for the escape into addiction—and the vicious cycle continues.

I have worked with many individuals who are deeply in love with people who were both unable to return that love and unwilling to do what it took to gain the necessary freedom and skill to love. No matter how much they reached out to their partners, no matter what they were willing to do, no matter how much they were willing to go the extra mile, it made no difference. Yet the unrealistic expectations continued. They continued to expect their partners, who were still rooted in their addictions, to speak rationally, tell the truth, be willing to play fair. They never did because they could not.

As I have repeatedly said throughout this book, just because you don't have a skill doesn't mean you can't develop it. Until there is evidence, however, that someone's putting out the effort to grow, it is a fool's errand to count on a healthy, loving response from a person who does not have it to give. Sooner or later, no matter how deep the love, resentment will replace hope, anger will replace patience, and hatred will replace hospitality. But how fair is it to demand something that your partner can't give and then seek revenge when it's not given?

If you are involved with someone who doesn't have the skills necessary for a nurturing relationship, you need to realize that your partner will probably be more than content to let things continue as long as you are willing. That leaves you to act. There is nothing worse in a relationship than to assume the role of victim. Victims are people who think they have no choices. They perceive themselves as powerless and unable to make decisions. But there are always choices. They may not be the choices you want, and there may be no decisions that do not hurt, but there are always choices. It is critical that each individual retains the ability to choose. No one does it to us; we are not here because we have no other choice. We are here because we choose to be.

In, Out, or Wait

An individual can occupy only three places in a relationship: In, Out, or Wait.

In means that both individuals want to be in the relationship and are working in a constructive way to build the trust and hospitality necessary.

Out means that one or the other or both—it only takes one—has decided to get out. For whatever reason or set of reasons, one partner has "fallen out of love" and does not want to be or is not willing to try to be in the relationship. No matter how much you may love someone who chooses Out, if that is the choice, you do not have a choice about being In. If your partner is Out, then so are you; and your choice here is not about the relationship but about your reaction to your partner's decision. You can choose to continue chasing him or her, trying to force your partner to choose In; you can choose to remain depressed and bitter; you can choose to withdraw into isolation and separation for the rest of your life. Or you can choose something else. You can choose the opposite. No matter how unfair you think it is, no matter how justified you are in being bitter or withdrawn, no matter how hard it is to let go and move on, you can choose to do just that.

Wait, the third option, is a valid choice. Wait means I know I am not happy now, I recognize that my needs are not being met, and I am not willing to live this way forever, but neither am I willing or ready to walk away. So I choose to gamble. I choose to stay right here doing what I can to create an environment most conducive to my partner's growth and change.

This is a valid choice, but many people subconsciously choose willed confusion instead. They seem to stumble around, not knowing why things are the way they are or what to do about it. Confusion, of course, is a marvelous way to avoid decisions. If we are confused enough, how can anyone, including ourselves, expect us to make a decision? But confusion hurts; and when we choose it, we sacrifice all power to influence our loved one.

Choosing Wait in a conscious, up-front, straight-thinking way is infinitely superior to choosing willed confusion. When we choose Wait, however, we own that it is temporary, since it cannot go on forever; and we own that by choosing it we retain our own power—it is our decision to be here, so we should stop complaining about all that is wrong in our relationship! If it gets bad enough and we are no longer willing to put up with it, we can always choose Out. It's up to us.

If you are stuck in Wait, you can still keep busy. Doing what? You can (1) understand; (2) decide; (3) work your own program; (4) refuse to enable or to seek revenge; (5) create a crisis; or (6) if it is over, walk away and never look back. Let's take a closer look at each of these options.

Understand

It has been said that no one *wants* to be a jerk. If you are in a relationship with someone who does not play fair and in so doing causes you much pain, understand that there are reasons. Not that there aren't also choices, but there are reasons. The more effort you exert to understand those reasons—family-of-origin reasons, life experience reasons—the more beneficial it will be.

This is not to say, of course, that the more you understand the more you should be willing to accept intolerable behavior. No. But the more understanding you possess, the better equipped you are to act in a way that might help.

Also, the more understanding you gain the less angry you may become. As irritating and frustrating as your partner's behavior may be, at least you see a reason for its existence. From your new perspective, you may be better able to say something in a different tone of voice, with a look in your eye that encourages rather than rejects.

Decide

Again, it's important not to allow yourself to be a victim who has no power and no ability to make decisions. You can decide In, Out, or Wait. You can decide how long you are willing to Wait. You can decide what it really is you want for your life, you can decide what it is costing you and will cost you if you refuse to decide. You have many, many choices. All of them—when you make them—can empower you.

Work Your Own Program

More will be said about working your own program in the next chapter. Basically, it means to take care of yourself. There is no greater gift you can give your partner and no more powerful thing you can do for your relationship than to be as healthy as you possibly can be. How effective you are in encouraging good in your relationship is directly proportional to the degree of serenity and balance you possess.

When we are in pain our first impulse is to withdraw and retreat, to stop doing everything that gave us pleasure before. We discontinue hobbies, overlook friends, and neglect having fun. But the more depleted we become, the less we have to give.

To take care of yourself you need to be willing to ask the tough questions. Self-delusion is no gift to yourself. If you have chosen Wait, regularly ask yourself these questions: Is this where I want to be? Is all this uncertainty worth it? Is this where my partner wants to be? How long am I willing to wait?

At first glance asking the tough questions may not seem to be a good way to take care of yourself. They may hurt. The fact is, however, that it eventually hurts far more *not* to ask these questions, because the down side of choosing Wait—the uncertainty—can kill you.

Refuse to Enable or to Seek Revenge

While you're in Wait, it is difficult not to choose one of these paths. More common is to switch back and forth between the two, creating more confusion and conflict as you do so.

To "enable" means to be overly willing to do anything to keep your partner happy, often in response to the panic you may feel that your relationship may end and you may end up alone. Enablers will make excuses for and accept excuses from their partners. They will accept intolerable behavior, smile when they want to cry, and refuse to look honestly at the direction the relationship is going. Whenever Enablers enable they send out the message that whatever their partners choose to do is okay; there will be no consequence. By continuing the behavior that got them in Wait in the first place, Enablers create all the more pressure and confusion.

Another option during Wait involves the opposite behavior: to quit trying, but not to choose Out. And what do people do who stay stuck in Wait when the relationship has ended? They get revenge. The ways of getting revenge, of course, are endless. Sly putdowns, cynicism, deliberately choosing anything that's contrary to what the partner says or does. Revenge is a game, like all the others; and game responds to game.

Only by asking the tough questions and working a personal program can a person stuck in Wait avoid falling into these traps.

Create a Crisis

Getting out of Wait and into In or Out often requires a crisis. Someone must say, "It's over," or "I am not willing to live this way any longer. Here is what must happen or it is over."

Creating a crisis is a last-ditch technique. Don't do it unless you are certain you can live with the consequences. Here are the four phases you must act out to successfully create a crisis:

1. *State your demands clearly and specifically.* Generalities don't work here. A hopelessly general demand, like "respect me" or "care for me," leaves the door wide open for more delusion. A clearly stated demand is much more specific: "It is simply not acceptable to me that you continually spend money that we do not have. I can't live with that. It makes me feel like a failure and totally powerless in our relationship. I need to have a say in our decision to spend any significant amount of money." Realize that although you may want your partner's attitude to change, because it's the attitude beneath the behavior that counts, it is extremely difficult to monitor attitudes. But you can keep track of behaviors, which are the proof of attitude. Anyone can say or promise anything. But are those words and promises backed up by actions?

2. *State the consequences clearly.* Demands without consequences are powerless. If there are no consequences, why would anyone respond? The consequences need to be as clear and as clearly stated as the demands. Merely saying "or something terrible will happen" carries little power. On the other hand, announcing that, "If these demands of mine are not met in two weeks, then I will contact the lawyer" leaves little doubt. It's clear. What is being asked for is clear and the consequence of not responding is clear. Do you have a right to *demand* anything of your partner in a relationship? You sure do. Remember the tennis match? *You* are one-half of the game. You have every right to demand what is essential to you. You have every right to set the limits of what you are willing to live with and what you are not.

3. *Put a monitoring system in place.* Again, it's easy to make promises, and it's easy to make temporary alterations in behavior. But more than one "crisis creator" has been lulled to sleep by the temporary compliance of a partner, only to find

out that it was all a game. Two weeks later, inch by inch, things were back to what they were before. Nothing had changed. A monitoring system had been overlooked. A good system most often involves a weekly check-up, a specific time set aside when the parties are free to talk with one another and check on the specific behavior—either your partner is sober or not, either the signs of infidelity have disappeared or they haven't. It can also be a marvelous time for dialogue. If you're acting out healthy, trusting behavior, share with each other how it feels. Talk about whether this path feels better than the old one. Just talk!

4. *Make sure you consistently apply the consequences.* The worst possible mistake is to back down on the consequences. When you don't immediately and consistently enforce the consequences, you are clearly saying, "I don't really mean this, and you don't have to pay any attention." Don't worry, your partner won't. You must be willing to follow through and live with the consequences you determine in advance. Thus people in Wait have an enormous need for a support system and a personal program growth. It takes a great deal of strength to be in Wait and not disintegrate. It also takes a great deal of strength to create a crisis and stick with the consequences. Even though you may know right down to your toes that what you're doing is both necessary and right, being right doesn't make it easy.

If It Is Over, Walk Away and Never Look Back

This last point is not easy, just essential. If you have created a crisis or have come to the realization that it is over, then the only step possible is closure. Closure means you have chosen Out. It doesn't mean maybe, it doesn't mean the door is open a little, it doesn't mean, "Unless there's change I am through." All of those may be valid, but they define Wait. When you know it's over or when you choose it to be over, the only fair, sane decision left is Out. Out means that the relationship is dead.

Out does not mean you still don't care about the other person. It doesn't mean that all the feelings are dead, though they may be. What it does mean is you are no longer involved in the relationship. Closure means that with all the sadness and grief that may accompany it, you are no longer willing to try, that the door is shut, and that you are looking forward with your life.

If you have remained emotionally attached to your partner and your partner wants out, chances are he or she may offer to still be friends. In what seems to be a spirit of forgiveness and maturity, you may be invited to stay in touch, have coffee once in a while, perhaps even double-date now that the relationship is over. Beware! If you are emotionally attached, you cannot possibly have periodic contact with this person and still find freedom. After enough time has passed maybe you will, but not now. Such offers are more often than not an attempt to soothe feelings of guilt, not an attempt to be friends. If friendship is the issue, be a friend to yourself first. Refuse to put yourself in a lose-lose situation where your heart can break a little more.

There is nothing easy about Out or Wait, and certainly nothing easy about getting closure, but it's important not to do or believe the things that will make the experience even harder than it already is. The sooner we start to heal, the sooner we can get past the painful present and work for a better tomorrow. I hope these suggestions will speed up that process.

Straight Talk

The bottom line for all relationships is straight talk and straight walk—what we say and what we do. When people don't talk straight, you can't make clear decisions because you can't trust what they say. First they say one thing, then another. What was firm yesterday is smoke today. Promises evaporate. Insanity becomes the norm.

There are many reasons why people talk crooked, of course. Somtimes they are on chemicals. Sometimes they are so stuck in a People-Pleasing pattern that they simply can't tell the truth. In an effort to hurt no one they hurt everyone. Sometimes crooked talkers just get so exhausted from trying to live out their tangled lives that another lie seems easier than telling the truth and taking the consequences. Sometimes crooked talkers just don't care; they maintain an emotional distance from any and all relationships so if they hurt someone in the confusion, they can detach and, in a dead sort of way, move on to the next relationship.

Whatever the reasons, *only straight talk works*, whether you use it to work for a healthy, living relationship or to end a deadly, toxic one.

You deserve straight talk, so demand it.

Your partner deserves straight talk, so give it.

Chapter 7

A PERSONAL PROGRAM OF GROWTH

I've said it many times: "If nothing changes, nothing changes." That is a simple sentence, yet it contains a profound and deep thought. Change will not occur by itself. You must do something different for results to be different. Insanity has been wonderfully defined as expecting different results from the same behavior. The result of repeating the same behaviors over and over again is that nothing will change in your life. Change means doing something new; change means growth.

As I have described it in *Stage II Recovery*, all change happens in three steps: through conversion, decision, and program. You have a *conversion* when you recognize that enough is enough; or that it hurts too much to continue to be the way you are; or that you are beating your head against a wall, and that if you continue on this path, you will lose something or someone (like your health, your integrity, your self-esteem, your kids, or your relationship) you are not prepared to live without. Until conversion occurs, there will be no change; and unless you undergo a really profound conversion experience, a total act of your will to make things different, nothing will change.

Decision is the next step. It is one thing to have the conversion experience in your life, but now what are you going to do about it? You have recognized that if you continue on the path you are on, you are going to lose something of value to you. But you will lose it unless you consciously *decide* to change. Making a decision to change means giving up the old habits that are deeply ingrained in you, habits you have practiced all of your life. You have gained the insight to recognize that you have to make a change in your life, but how do you go about making the change? You must first *decide* that things will be different in your life.

I decided to make some change in my life when I had hit bottom. My bottom was watching my father die of a heart attack and realizing that I felt nothing. All my life I had practiced stuffing my feelings or denying them. There I was, my father was dying in front of my eyes, and I felt nothing except numb. All of a sudden it hit me that if I didn't do something to change, I would die before I really knew what it was like to live. It scared me so much to realize that I didn't feel anything, that I was numb, that I didn't even know what love really was. It was then that I knew something had to be different. I had to change, because I was not willing to live the rest of my life numb and unfeeling. What is your bottom? What will make you decide to change?

The most important element in achieving change is a personal program structured specifically to reach and maintain your desired goals. What is a program? It is simply practicing new skills.

Constructing a Program for Change

The quality of a personal program is going to dictate the quality of the person and the quality of any relationship that person is in. We work a program to overcome that which is causing us so much pain that we can no longer tolerate it. We work a program to get healthy and stay that way—spiritually, physically, and emotionally. Each of us can work only our own program. *My* program can only succeed because *I* own it and *I* choose to do it. Likewise for your program.

Three qualities are required if a program is to be effective. One, the program must be *concrete*: It must specify who, when, where, and what, or it will not be effective. Two, it must be *practical*: You must be able to do it; it must go in a specific direction; and you are accountable for end results. Three, it must be *focused*: It must have a specific emphasis so that it's obvious what you're working on.

With those criteria in mind, we can now look at how to construct a program for change and improvement.

Your Personal Growth

In chapter 2, I stressed an important principle about relationships: They can only be as healthy as the people involved in them. Both people in the relationship must be willing to deal with the self-defeating behaviors that are getting in the way of their relationship and preventing it from being as happy and as healthy as it could be. This means that *you* must be willing to work on your own program of growth and change in order to stop practicing the same old habits. You are the only person who can take responsibility for your actions and change your habits.

What habits do you need to change? A good place to start is to make a list of habits you want to stop and a list of habits you want to start practicing. Take a piece of paper and draw a large "T" on it. On the left side of the "T" write "stop"; on the right side write "start."

To help you get started on your lists, let's look at some habits other people have decided they must change.

- *Stay away from slippery places.* Slippery places are those which can cause you to slip back into old habits and self-defeating behaviors. Some slippery places might be bars, family or holiday gatherings, race tracks, annual trips to Las Vegas.
- *Stay away from slippery actions.* Starting affairs or new romances, overeating, overspending, oversmoking, lying, deluding yourself, making excuses, "awfulizing" (making things worse than they are), overworking, overworrying, blaming others.
- *Stay away from habits that harm your relationship and hurt you.* Getting involved in lose-lose relationships with people who have no capacity to make them work; not being trust-

worthy; pitying or feeling sorry for yourself; taking a job you are not qualified for; rationalizing that your life is just bad luck and there is nothing you can do about it; letting other people use you because you won't say no; projecting—saying life would be better "if only . . ."; being financially irresponsible—either overspending or underspending.

What sorts of self-defeating habits are you practicing? Spend some time developing your "stop" list. Now, what do you have to "start" doing? In many cases, of course, what you have to start doing is the opposite of what you decided to stop doing. For example, perhaps you listed "stop going to family gatherings." Then, what do you start? You start by saying no the next time you are invited to one. You can do a lot to change your self-defeating habits and become a person capable of functioning in healthy relationships. For example:

- *Share.* You need to learn to share who you are. If you want a relationship with a healthy person, that person will want to know who you are, will want to share himself or herself with you and will want you to do the same.
- *Stick with winners.* Define who a "winner" is for you. You might decide that winners are people who are honest, who share themselves with others, who feel positive about life and living, who are happy, and who enjoy life without being irresponsible. Doesn't it say a lot about you if you don't know any people like that? Find some winners—there are plenty of them around—and then stick with them.
- *Celebrate.* That doesn't mean party all the time. It means to affirm yourself in your heart. Pat yourself on the back when you accomplish something new, however small you may think it is. Affirm yourself, celebrate your small victories over your self-defeating habits.
- *Have fun.* Even if you are broke, there are a lot of free places to go to give yourself a change of scenery.
- *Take care of yourself physically.* Start a regular program of ex-

ercise. Improve your diet. If you are junked up on caffeine, sugar, and fast foods, you are depleting the energy your body needs to fight the war against the habits you have practiced for years.[5]

• *Pray.* Prayer starts where your power ends.

• *Meditate.* Meditating is being quiet enough so you can listen. Meditation is slowing yourself down so you can listen to what's inside of you.

• *Be financially responsible.* Poor financial management really puts pressure on people. Perhaps you need to start budgeting, or saving, or spending. Work this out as it applies directly to you—what do you need to do to be more financially responsible?

Developing a stop-and-start list is not really difficult. We all know what we should or should not be doing. The difficult task is to start practicing our list, really stop doing some things and start doing others. What will help you in this difficult task? You must have a good support system.

A support system, consisting of a sponsor, a group, and a higher power, will help you to continue on your path toward personal growth and change.

A *sponsor* should be someone of the same sex who has expertise in areas that are important to you, has strengths where you have weaknesses, is willing to share with you, and has no need either to put you on a pedestal or tear you down.

A *group* will provide you with an opportunity to share and learn from the experiences of other people. You learn, as Carl Jung has said, "That which is most personal is most common." In other words, the deepest, darkest secrets that you keep inside of you are the same deep and dark secrets everyone else has. If you hide your fears, your wants, and your needs deep inside, you'll find in group that others also have fears, wants, and needs deep inside that they keep hidden. A group provides you with acceptance, support, challenge, and love.

A *higher power,* or God as you understand God to be, will give you the opportunity to accept yourself as a worthy and loved individual. The first thing God asks of you is to accept that you are loved. When you can accept that, you have the opportunity to become all that you can be. If you can accept love, you can give love—the essential ingredient of a healthy relationship with another person.

It takes a great deal of energy and personal psychological freedom to function in healthy relationships. A program for your own personal growth is essential as a prerequisite to developing a program of building and improving your relationships with others. I've said before that a relationship is like a tightrope, and a tightrope is only as strong as the two poles supporting it. As one pole in your relationship, you need to develop the maturity and strength necessary to take care of yourself, since you can only give to your relationship what you have and who you are. Having your own program for growth is the first step in making your relationships better.

Your Growth as a Couple

Working a program for your own personal growth is extremely important. If both you and your partner are working your own individual programs, you might assume that the difficulties between you would simply disappear. Unfortunately, this is not correct. There have been instances where both people were successfully working their own programs, but their marriage ended. As much as it is important to work on changing yourself and how you relate to each other, it is equally important to develop a program for your relationship.

A program, as we have defined it, is a series of small behaviors. A program for couples consists of a series of small behaviors that are designed to enhance the relationship, develop honest communication and trust, and strengthen the bonds between the individuals. The following program of coupling involves being very specific and disciplined about five basic areas that are important for establishing closeness.

1. *Dates.* It has been my experience that once a relationship has been formed, some or all of the fun often goes out of it. During the courtship phase, fun was the main agenda; but once that phase is over, the fun disappears and is replaced by responsibility and problems. Your partner may come to represent those two grim realities, and if that's your perception, you may hesitate to spend too much time with him or her. Disciplining yourself so that dates—which should equal fun—are a constant part of your life together is essential. Make a rule that no work and no problems are to be talked about on your dates. This is *fun* time. You may discover that you have lost the ability to have fun, but that discovery is worth its weight in gold. If it *is* true, it is time to start learning how to enjoy life together once more.

2. *Dialogue.* In dialogue you're neither solving problems nor just passing time with each other. The purpose of dialogue is to understand more fully who your partner is. Although it may be fun, it is focused and directed, and it's done with a purpose. Remember, more often than not in a relationship it is the woman—who was reared with permission to share, with a hunger for revelation, with a great delight in talking about feelings—who will passionately espouse dialogue. A man may find it much more difficult. Unlike a woman, he may not only *not* have the necessary skills, but may in fact have fearsome hurdles to cross. Hospitality is the word here.

In your quest for improved dialogue, do not become your own worst enemy by demanding too much too soon or by discounting any progress made because it is too small. Go slowly and offer lots of encouragement so your partner need not hide behind old barricades such as, "It's just me. Take it or leave it." Or, "I can't help it. I was raised that way." Just last night, I heard someone say, "God loves us just the way we are, but he loves us too much to let us stay that way."

Any of the previously outlined communication techniques (pages 83 to 86) can serve as tools for dialogue.

3. *Problem solving.* Problem solving means finding resolution for what ails us. It has been said that we are only as sick as our secrets. In the same vein it is the problems not faced that loom the largest. Mice become lions in the dark. Once we haul them out into the light, they usually shrink. Even if they don't, they become much less fearsome.

My wife and I have found that setting aside a specific time for problem solving each week frees up much time that would otherwise be spent running from a problem. Our problem-solving time is Saturday. Knowing that we have set aside a specific time for dealing with our problems allows us to avoid feeling that these issues are just hiding in the background, growing each day. Often enough the issues deal with scheduling rides, paying bills, manipulating the calendar. Obviously, if there's a major crisis, we don't wait till Saturday; but you will be surprised at how many things can be put off and then dealt with. Once dealt with they are gone.

4. *Meals.* In our busy world, many families have meals together infrequently. And if meals are not just a time to eat, but a time to share with each other, when does that get done? When do we find out what is going on in each other's lives? When is there time or opportunity for the support, encouragement, and praise that should be a part of family life and build the hospitality that families need? Maybe not all families can eat together, at least not regularly; but some other time for the members of a family to interact needs to be found. Every day our children are learning what *family* means by observing and being around the family we provide.

5. *Prayer.* Prayer, of course, is personal. The various ways couples and families find to pray are best left to their own creativity. Some are most comfortable with a formal reading from the Bible or some spiritual literature followed by spontaneous or formalized prayer. Some couples function best in strict informality. Some find it helpful, at least for now, to pray in the dark. I know many couples who pray best just before going

to sleep. They hold hands and spontaneously thank God for the daily blessings and ask for assistance for the future. The fact is, it is hard to fight with someone you pray with. Prayer, among many other things, is a cement and a glue that holds people together.

These five specific behaviors are important to include in your program for you and your partner. Remember that it takes action on the part of both people to make the relationship grow and improve. An unending series of excuses and reasons why one or all of the behaviors can't take place is a pretty clear indication that the relationship is not going to work. However, if you will do these activities in a regular, consistent, and structured way, there is no end to the potential for growth of the relationship.

To make sure these are more than just good ideas, I suggest you use the following graph to fill in the specifics. All five may not fit, and other activities may be more important to you. The point is that whatever you chose, whatever activities you build your relationship on, you must do them consistently. Know when they are going to happen.

	When	Where
Dates		
Dialogue		
Problem solving		
Meals		
Prayer		

I can't say, "Be patient, go slow," often enough! No one and no program is perfect. We make mistakes. At times we are downright deceitful and we know it. That does not necessarily mean you should terminate your relationship. It does argue for the necessity of personal growth. If our partners are trying as best they can, we should congratulate them on their effort and encourage them to continue. More ground will be won by attraction than ever was won by nagging and pushing.

Chapter 8

THE CHALLENGE AHEAD

I once heard someone say, "There is no such thing as an ending; the end of something is simply the opportunity for a new beginning." I would like you to think of coming to the end of this book on Stage II relationships as the opportunity for a new beginning. Thousands of people have undertaken this journey of "learning to love." Their journeys have not been easy, since the road to recovery is long and hard, full of potholes, detours, construction zones, closed bridges, and dead ends. But all of these people have found that their willingness, determination, consistency, and effort have produced the results they desired: They have recovered from their codependency and have learned to love in a fully human and divine way.

What lies ahead for you? Are you willing to accept the challenge of the tasks of Stage II relationships? Are you willing to take the risks, endure the pain, accept the consequences? Are you willing to accept the fact that the only thing preventing you from leading a happier life, filled with a loving relationship, is yourself? Can you acknowledge the fact that you have the opportunity to change? That you are limited only by your attitudes and not by opportunity?

Have you experienced your conversion? Have you recognized—deep inside—that if you do not change you are going to lose something of great value? If so, you need to decide to act. You need to accept the challenge to change and begin to take those necessary steps to initiate that change.

I shared with you the moment of my conversion—when I

watched my father dying and felt nothing. At that time I needed to change, and I knew it. But a long period of time elapsed between my conversion and my decision to act because I didn't know what to do about changing. I didn't know how to begin my own program of recovery.

If you have read this book thoroughly, you have learned how to construct your own program for personal growth. You know how to begin and how to proceed. You need only the willingness to decide to act, the determination to proceed and succeed. Your attitude is the only thing preventing you from achieving your own personal growth. Your *attitude*—not opportunity, not other people, not your life problems, not your family background, not your education, or any other of the many excuses we can find—is all that stands in the way of accepting the challenge.

A Plan for Sane Living

I would like to share with you a ten-point plan for sane living. These ten points, if practiced, will help you to change your attitude toward yourself, your life, and the challenges that face you. If you practice these ten points, even in the roughest of times in your life, you will feel more sane, more serene, more loved and loving.

1. *Believe that life is meant to be good.* Not bad, not awful, not full of consistent pain, but *good.* Life is meant to be a celebration and you can learn to celebrate life.
2. *Decisions are demanded of you.* Whatever the consequences in your life, they are a direct reflection of the decisions you make. It is not relevant whether the decisions are easy or hard, whether you want or do not want to make them, whether or not it is fair. The fact still remains that you will have to make decisions.
3. *There are no accidents.* By and large, what happens in your life is not accidental—it's a matter of the choices you make or fail to make. The more you are willing to take a look at your life, the more you will be in control of it.

4. *You count. You are important.* You must be willing to take care of yourself first, so you are able to be a person who radiates health and wholeness.

5. *Others count.* You must accept that others are also important.

6. *Feelings alone cannot dictate your behavior.* It is important to know how you feel, but you cannot let how you feel dictate your behavior and your decisions.

7. *Refuse to be the agent of your own unhappiness.* Each of us can be our own worst enemy. By looking carefully at your life, you can choose how you feel about it. You can be as happy as you choose to be.

8. *You are responsible only for yourself.* Learn that there are boundaries between yourself and others. Let go of your need to "caretake" others and learn to be responsible only for yourself.

9. *Act consistently.* Whatever skills you develop in your life are the result of consistent habits. Just stopping one behavior and starting another does not guarantee the results you want. Healthy, sane behavior is the result of acting *consistently* in a healthy way.

10. *You cannot do it alone.* Certainly no one else can grow and change for you, only you can accomplish that. But it is a deeply ingrained spiritual truth that you are not a solitary being. You need a support system; friends, sharing, a higher power. You cannot walk alone. You need others.

Do you remember the letter from Jenny A. that opened this book? I'd like to quote from it again. She writes:

I found that we may come from slightly different places, *but we are all the same.* The same living issues—exactly the same issues—keep surfacing in all these different kinds of meetings. We are all lonely. We are all stopped by the glass wall. We are all deficient in the skills we need to have healthy relationships.

So now my effort and energy in recovery are much more focused on getting rid of the glass wall. Slowly, because it is *so* scary, I am learning what I need to do to connect with others. *Mostly it has to do with changing my own attitudes and perceptions*. But I am learning, and my life is so much "warmer," so to speak, because I am getting closer to people.

Learning to love means learning new skills, giving up old habits, learning about myself, working a program of personal growth, and changing the attitudes and perceptions you have held for much of your life. The challenge of your new beginning is there in front of you.

NOTES

1. Caretakers, as I have described them in Earnie Larsen, *Stage II Recovery* (San Francisco: Harper & Row, 1985, 21–22) and in this book on pages 60–62, are dependent on their need to do things for other people, and they generally feel responsible for the happiness of others.
2. In a somewhat different context, the psychologist Abraham Maslow used a pyramid to illustrate a hierarchy of needs he had identified. Although I'm not describing exactly the same needs, the pyramid is a useful graphic model.
3. A complete discussion of habits can be found in Earnie Larsen, *Stage II Recovery* (San Francisco: Harper & Row, 1985), 30–45.
4. More detailed descriptions of each pattern can be found in Larsen, *Stage II Recovery*, 19–29.
5. For a discussion of the energy depletion cycle and the importance of exercise and healthy diet to recovery and your life attitude, you may want to listen to a six-tape cassette series I've prepared, called *How to Keep Your Balance in a Rocking Boat*. For more information, write E. Larsen Enterprises, 7549 Douglas Dr. N., Brooklyn Park, MN 55443.